Cambridge Elements ≡

Elements in the Problems of God
edited by
Michael L. Peterson
Asbury Theological Seminary

CHRISTIAN PHILOSOPHY AND THE PROBLEM OF GOD

Charles Taliaferro
St. Olaf College

CAMBRIDGE
UNIVERSITY PRESS

Shaftesbury Road, Cambridge CB2 8EA, United Kingdom

One Liberty Plaza, 20th Floor, New York, NY 10006, USA

477 Williamstown Road, Port Melbourne, VIC 3207, Australia

314–321, 3rd Floor, Plot 3, Splendor Forum, Jasola District Centre,
New Delhi – 110025, India

103 Penang Road, #05–06/07, Visioncrest Commercial, Singapore 238467

Cambridge University Press is part of Cambridge University Press & Assessment,
a department of the University of Cambridge.

We share the University's mission to contribute to society through the pursuit of
education, learning and research at the highest international levels of excellence.

www.cambridge.org
Information on this title: www.cambridge.org/9781009296069

DOI: 10.1017/9781009296045

© Charles Taliaferro 2023

This publication is in copyright. Subject to statutory exception and to the provisions
of relevant collective licensing agreements, no reproduction of any part may take
place without the written permission of Cambridge University Press & Assessment.

First published 2023

A catalogue record for this publication is available from the British Library.

ISBN 978-1-009-29606-9 Paperback
ISSN 2754-8724 (online)
ISSN 2754-8716 (print)

Cambridge University Press & Assessment has no responsibility for the persistence
or accuracy of URLs for external or third-party internet websites referred to in this
publication and does not guarantee that any content on such websites is, or will
remain, accurate or appropriate.

Christian Philosophy and the Problem of God

Elements in the Problems of God

DOI: 10.1017/9781009296045
First published online: June 2023

Charles Taliaferro
St. Olaf College

Author for correspondence: Charles Taliaferro, taliafer@stolaf.edu

Abstract: Questions are raised about Christian philosophy and God. Is Christian philosophy truly philosophical? Is it biblical? Is it capable of addressing God, a profoundly transcendent being? Does appealing to a God's-eye point of view make sense? Can Christian philosophy respect religious diversity? While the integrity of Christian philosophy is defended, questions are raised about its relationship to the overall practice of philosophy. Christian philosophers value drawing others to Christian faith. Are Christian apologetics compatible with philosophy? This Element concludes with reflections on when it may be philosophically acceptable to appeal to mystery.

Keywords: evidence, faith, problem of evil, God's-eye point of view, transcendence

© Charles Taliaferro 2023

ISBNs: 9781009296069 (PB), 9781009296045 (OC)
ISSNs: 2754-8724 (online), 2754-8716 (print)

Contents

1 Is "Christian Philosophy" a Problem?

"Christian philosophy" is not an everyday term; it does not appear in most current dictionaries and encyclopedias of philosophy. When I used the term to register for a year of residential study in Great Britain, I was told by an officer that it was a *funny term*. He knew about Christianity, philosophy, religion, and Christian theology, but "'Christian philosophy'? Isn't that a misnomer or contradiction in terms?" If that officer or any other member of Oxford's Thames Valley Police is reading this, please keep reading.

In this Element, I use the term "Christian philosophy" in accord with books like the *History of Christian Philosophy in the Middle Ages* by Étienne Gilson and as the term is used by today's Society of Christian Philosophers (SCP). Broadly speaking, Christian philosophy is philosophical work done mostly by Christians about the nature and practice of Christianity, its justification, its relation to other religions and to secular naturalism, Christian conceptions of good and evil, forgiveness and redemption, justice and mercy, Christian ethical theory and applied ethics (medical ethics, environmental ethics, etc.), belief in the Trinity, the Incarnation, the experience of God, the practices of prayer, worship, social activism, and more. Following the SCP, I shall not assume Christian philosophy is Roman Catholic, Anglican, Protestant, or Eastern Orthodox or that it reflects any particular denomination or communion – unlike philosophy fostered by the American Catholic Association, which is Roman Catholic, or the Evangelical Philosophical Society, which is mostly but not exclusively Protestant. As the term is used in this Element, Christian philosophy is mostly practiced by Christians, but there is no reason whatever why non-Christians cannot contribute to Christian philosophy. This is not merely hypothetical; over many years, non-Christian philosophers like William Rowe and John Fischer have made brilliant contributions to Christian philosophy (perhaps this is why Rowe referred to his own philosophy as *friendly* atheism). A self-identified agnostic (in this case, someone who professes not to know whether God exists), Robin Le Poidevin, has just published an intricate, well-argued case for the credibility of belief in the Incarnation, called *And Was Made Man: Mind, Metaphysics, and Incarnation* (Le Poidevin 2023).[1] This openness to contributing to Christian philosophy by atheists and agnostics reflects today's (mostly) friendly intellectual climate in which non-Muslims contribute to Islamic philosophy, non-Buddhists contribute to Buddhist philosophy, and so on. Actually, the history of

---

[1] This Element will not be heavily laden with terminology and hyper-analytical definitions, but I note that while the term "agnostic" is often used today to refer to persons not committed to affirming or denying X (say, Christianity), it can apply to persons who affirm a position but do not claim *to know with certainty that the position is true*. On such a definition, persons may be agnostic and practicing Christians on the grounds that they believe (perhaps for good reasons) that Christianity is true, but do not profess to know that it is true.

philosophy itself is far more porous than it may appear on the surface. During the medieval era, there was a great deal of mutual influence and interaction between Jewish, Christian, and Islamic thinkers, especially over their engagement with ancient and classical Greco-Roman thought. Today, there are many projects involving dialogues with diverse religious and secular philosophers.[2]

Why care about Christian philosophy? Christianity is diverse with multiple communal traditions, but its common vision of God as the limitlessly powerful, loving, omnipresent, good creator and redeemer of the world has captured the imagination and energy of abundant philosophers since the beginning of Christianity in the first century. One Christian philosopher has even argued that there is reason to hope that the God of Christianity exists.

> Why hope that there is a God? Because of compassion for those who have suffered innocently; because of desire that their suffering not have been useless and terminal, i.e., redeemable after death. As long as it is logically possible that evil be defeated, that innocent suffering is not meaningless and final, it seems to me that we have a moral obligation to hope that that possibility is actual. Therefore, we have a moral obligation to hope that there is a God because, if there is a God, then innocent suffering is not meaningless or final. (Creel 1986, 149)

Philosophically exploring the possible meaning(s) of life can naturally lead us to reflect on the plausibility of such religious conceptions of reality. One contemporary philosopher sees the role of philosophy in thoroughly secular terms: "There is exactly one overriding question in contemporary philosophy . . . How do we fit in? . . . How can we square this self-conception of ourselves as mindful, meaning-creating, free, rational, etc., agents with a universe that consists entirely of mindless, unfree, nonrational, brute physical particles?" (Searle 2007, 4).

Good question. But then there is also this question: is it possible or even reasonable to believe that reality is more than our view of "mindless, unfree, nonrational, brute physical particles"? I suggest that the many tasks of philosophy are incomplete unless they include engaging the great theistic traditions of the world, including Christianity.[3]

Because this Element is on *the problem* of God and Christian philosophy, I offer some reflections on the term "problem." I suggest that not all of what we call a problem is bad or undesirable. For example, writing this Element started out as a huge problem for me (in the undesirable sense) as I began the writing while in

---

[2] The diversity of Christian and non-Christian philosophy is evident in the recent four-volume *Encyclopedia of Philosophy of Religion* (Goetz and Taliaferro 2021).

[3] Other theistic traditions include Judaism, Islam, theistic Hinduism, Sikhism, the Bahai, and some Indigenous traditions in Africa. For an overview of world religions, see my book *Religions: A Quick Immersion* (Taliaferro 2021).

a hospital for two weeks, facing four operations. Writing a philosophy book under those dire circumstances did not become easier despite the surprising enthusiasm for philosophy among the hospital staff – one of my nurses even had a philosophical tattoo (her arm had a graphic, colored tattoo depicting Plato's allegory of the cave)![4] Authorship continued to be onerous until I was released from the hospital to take on a different sort of problem. Then, in a library unfettered by constant medical attention, I had to squarely face up to the problem of writing this Element with the arduous, forbidding goal of ensuring it is intellectually stimulating and enlivening for you, whether you are a Christian, a secular critic of Christianity, a practicing Buddhist, or simply not religiously affiliated ("spiritual but not religious"). Moreover, in order to reach the goal of publication, I had the problem of satisfying my officious yet noble editor and a band of anonymous (perhaps even ruthless) philosophical reviewers. This was decidedly (as my students would say) not easy-peasy, but it was and is a problem I welcomed and hoped to meet.

I concede that very often in English the term "problem" is used to refer only to undesirable obstacles. If you email me that you have five problems with this Element, at first I will assume the worst. But such negative usage is not always the case. In his famous book *The Problems of Philosophy*, Bertrand Russell identifies as philosophical problems those important quandaries that launch the very practice of philosophy.

> Is there any knowledge in the world which is so certain that no reasonable man could doubt it? This question, which at first sight might not seem difficult, is really one of the most difficult that can be asked. When we have realised the obstacles in the way of a straightforward and confident answer, we shall be well launched on the study of philosophy – for philosophy is merely the attempt to answer such ultimate questions, not carelessly and dogmatically, as we do in ordinary life and even in the sciences, but critically, after exploring all that makes such questions puzzling, and after realising all the vagueness and confusion that underlie our ordinary ideas. (Russell 1912, 1)

I cite Russell's *The Problems of Philosophy* not just as evidence that what are called problems can be beneficial but also to endorse his view that philosophical problems should be addressed with care, without dogmatism, and it sometimes involves questioning the assumptions we make in ordinary life. While I will part company with Russell later in this section on a different matter, I agree with his view that certain kinds of problems (questioning our ordinary claims about what we know about ourselves and the world) can launch philosophy – a task that (in my view) often requires imagination, time, and patience.

---

[4] For those interested in the philosophical significance of tattoos, see "Tattoos and the Tattooing Arts in Perspective" (Taliaferro and Odden 2012).

To summarize: while this work brings to light problems, some will be tagged undesirable while other problems may be thought desirable, perhaps providing occasions for creative philosophical developments. In what follows, let us consider some of what may be undesirable problems about the idea and practice of Christian philosophy.

1.1 Three Reasons to Be Suspicious about Christian Philosophy

Let us consider three claims that Christian philosophy is a vexing problem: (A) Christian faith does not appeal to evidence, whereas philosophy does. (B) The Bible is opposed to philosophy. (C) Christian philosophers are not really philosophers because they claim to know the answer to philosophical questions (like "Does God exist?") quite independent of (and perhaps prior to) engaging in philosophy. Some philosophers, including Russell, contend that true philosophers should not be constrained by independent answers to philosophical questions. At their best, philosophers should begin their practice by asking questions when they do not yet claim to know the answers to those questions

(A) *Faith and Evidence*. It has been claimed that Christianity is a matter of blind faith, whereas philosophy is not. Christians as well as non-Christians have described Christianity as a matter of having faith as opposed to relying on evidence or even having faith despite significant evidence against its truth. Separating religious faith from matters of evidence is not a merely marginal opinion, but seems to be officially adopted in the National Academy of Sciences and Institute of Medicine (now the National Academy of Medicine) statement on the relationship between science and religion:

> Science and religion are based on different aspects of human experience. In science, explanations must be based on evidence drawn from examining the natural world. Scientifically based observations or experiments that conflict with an explanation eventually must lead to modification or even abandonment of that explanation. Religious faith, in contrast, does not depend only on empirical evidence, is not necessarily modified in the face of conflicting evidence, and typically involves supernatural forces or entities. Because they are not a part of nature, supernatural entities cannot be investigated by science. In this sense, science and religion are separate and address aspects of human understanding in different ways. Attempts to pit science and religion against each other create controversy where none needs to exist. (NASIM 2008: 12)

At least at first glance, this statement appears to be conciliatory, aimed at defusing tension between religion and science, but it also may suggest that religious faith is inimical to both science and philosophy insofar as the latter are governed by evidence and reason.

The idea that Christianity is not a matter of evidence is sometimes advanced by hostile critics (I once heard an Ivy League philosophy professor remark that Christian faith involves people believing something that they know is false), but those sympathetic to Christianity have taken note of how much religious language does not function as though it involves a hypothesis based on evidence. For example, when Christians recite Psalm 23, they say, "The Lord is my shepherd," not "The Lord is probably my shepherd." The Christian creeds begin with a claim about what is believed but not a statement such as *we think it highly likely there is a God who created heaven and earth.*

Some argue that Christianity is more of a form of life in which people find meaning rather than adherence to a philosophical ontology (an account of what exists) or a scientific hypothesis. British philosopher of religion D. Z. Phillips contends that religious talk of the soul and religious practices such as prayer are best not thought of as people believing there are immaterial, ghostly substances called souls or that they are addressing an all-powerful bodiless person. According to Phillips, such language is better understood as ways that people express their love for one another and their solidarity in living with reverence. This may involve a kind of evidence – demonstrating in words and deeds that there is real love and solidarity – but not evidence for a hypothesis about the supernatural.

(B) *The Bible and philosophy.* There are biblical passages that suggest a negative view of philosophy. "See to it that no one takes you captive by philosophy and empty deceit, according to human tradition, according to the elemental spirits of the world, and not according to Christ" (Colossians 2:8). "And we impart this in words not taught by human wisdom but taught by the Spirit, interpreting spiritual truths to those who are spiritual" (1 Corinthians 2:13). "O Timothy, guard the deposit entrusted to you. Avoid the irreverent babble and contradictions of what is falsely called 'knowledge'" (1 Timothy 6:20).

While Christians differ (as we shall see) on the nature and interpretation of the Bible, it seems to many that the Bible has a highly authoritative role as a source for the knowledge (or awareness) of God. In the New Testament, we read that "All Scripture is inspired by God and beneficial for teaching, for rebuke, for correction, for training in righteousness" (2 Timothy 3:16). According to Romans 15:4, "For everything that was written in the past was written for our instruction, so that through endurance and the encouragement of the Scriptures, we might have hope." In 2 Peter 1:20–21, there is this affirmation: "Above all, you must understand that no prophecy of Scripture comes from one's own interpretation. For no such prophecy was ever brought forth by the will of man, but men spoke from God as they were carried along by the Holy Spirit." In light of these claims, shouldn't the Bible have primacy over philosophy or, more radically, shouldn't Scripture be the sole source of awareness of God as opposed to philosophy?

Some philosophers describe the task of philosophy as very much a matter of the free use of inquiry in which there is a reliance on our own reason rather than any traditional authority like the Bible or church tradition. Here is Immanuel Kant's famous account of what it is to be enlightened:

> Enlightenment is man's leaving his self-caused immaturity. Immaturity is the incapacity to use one's intelligence without the guidance of another. Such immaturity is self-caused if it is not caused by lack of intelligence, but by lack of determination and courage to use one's intelligence without being guided by another. *Sapere Aude!* [Dare to know!] Have the courage to use your own intelligence is therefore the motto of the enlightenment. (Kant 1784, 481)

While some Christians see the Bible as a primary, wise source of illumination, Kant contends that philosophers should engage in mature, courageous reflection themselves without relying on the guidance of others, including the guidance of the Bible itself. When we are immature children, the guidance of others is inevitable, maybe wise or prudent, but becoming mature involves thinking for oneself.

(C) *A philosophical problem with Christian philosophy.* Some philosophers contend that Christian faith stifles or subverts the practice of philosophy. Russell offered the following negative view of the philosophical standing of thirteenth-century Christian Thomas Aquinas, widely recognized by many Christian philosophers today, especially Roman Catholics, as an ideal philosopher.

> There is little of the true philosophic spirit in Aquinas. He does not, like the Platonic Socrates, set out to follow wherever the argument may lead. He is not engaged in an inquiry, the result of which it is impossible to know in advance. Before he begins to philosophize, he already knows the truth; it is declared in the Catholic faith. If he can find apparently rational arguments for some parts of the faith, so much the better; if he cannot, he need only fall back on revelation. The finding of arguments for a conclusion given in advance is not philosophy, but special pleading. I cannot, therefore, feel that he deserves to be put on a level with the best philosophers either of Greece or of modern times. (Russell 2009, 267; for a similar, more recent objection see Schellenberg 2019)

Let's now consider some replies to these objections.

1.2 Some Reasons to Welcome Christian Philosophy

Rely to A. First, some terminology. The notion that faith alone is key to Christianity has sometimes been referred to as *sola fide* (Latin for "faith alone") and some religious philosophers adopt what is called *fideism* (which might be called "faith-ism"). The opposite of fideism is often called *evidentialism*. According to a stringent version of evidentialism, it is always wrong to have a belief without good evidence. Here is the classic example of evidentialism by William Clifford in 1877: "It is wrong always, everywhere, and for anyone to believe anything on insufficient evidence."

The simplest reply to this first objection is that not all Christian philosophers adopt *sola fide* or fideism. In fact, many Christian philosophers, historically and today, are evidentialists; they argue that there is good, sufficient evidence on behalf of Christian beliefs. Some of this evidence is based on observations of the cosmos (its existence, stable natural laws enabling galaxies with their virtually uncountable stars and planets, the emergence of life, including the emergence of conscious, sentient beings who have free will, moral experiences, and so on). Some evidence is especially conceptual (as in the ontological argument, which takes as its starting point the idea of God as maximally excellent) while other evidential elements are experiential (widespread testimony about the ostensible experience of a divine reality across cultures and times).[5] In short, Christian philosophers from Thomas Aquinas to John Locke (eighteenth century) to today's Richard Swinburne and Andrew Loke do not rely on "blind faith."[6]

On religious language and practice: it would indeed be odd to say, "The Lord is probably my shepherd" or to introduce evidential language into creeds or reports of religious exchanges. But that does not mean that evidence is not involved. You would probably not tell someone "It is highly likely that I love you," even if you were not absolutely sure of your feelings and, in truth, you simply thought it very probable that you love the person. Christian language and practice often reflects trust in a relationship or what is believed to be affective responses to God involving worship, praise, veneration, petition, confession, and a variety of emotions like love, desire, fear, awe, dread, anger, and so on. Such acts and emotions would make little sense if the practitioner was convinced there is no God. Phillips has a point that often Christian language about God and the soul are about expressing love for, and solidarity with, others, but this talk is often predicated on the belief that there actually is a God and that persons are or have souls (some spiritual dimension).

As an aside, some critics of traditional Christianity use the term "supernatural" to refer to God and souls, but this term is not always helpful for three reasons: (i) "supernatural" refers to poltergeists, witches, goblins, and similar phenomena, and its use since the seventeenth century suggests "superstition";

---

[5] For a survey of this ostensible evidence, see the free, online *Stanford Encyclopedia of Philosophy* entry "Philosophy of Religion" (https://plato.stanford.edu/entries/philosophy-religion).

[6] What should be recognized, though, is that these Christian evidentialists include as evidence sources that go beyond the natural sciences. For example, they may appeal to philosophical arguments (not constrained by only empirical observation), the appeal to explanatory power, moral experience, values. For a superb book on the role of evidence in philosophy, see William Lycan's *On Evidence in Philosophy* (Lycan 2019).

(ii) according to much of traditional Christianity, God is natural (God has a nature), indeed God is the creative ground of the natural world (the cosmos); and (iii) many Christians see our souls as part of nature, the created order, and thus "natural." The traditional term for the God of Christianity in English for the past 350 years is *theism* (or its cognate, *theistic*).

A secondary reply to the first objection is also worth noting: evidentialism has itself been subjected to suspicion by both secular and religious philosophers. It has been difficult to arrive at a consensus about what counts as what Clifford refers to as "sufficient evidence." He cites an example of insufficient evidence (deeming a ship seaworthy on dodgy evidence, if any), but he does not provide a clear guide of when evidence is sufficient for a responsible belief. One of his critics, William James, pointed out how many of life's most important beliefs (e.g., the belief that life is worth living or that we have free will) are passionate in nature and do not leave us with decades to dispassionately weigh theoretical possibilities. The effort to restrict evidence to the empirical sciences alone has met with stiff resistance. Arguably, the empirical sciences seem not to account for mathematics and logic, subjective, conscious states and introspection, normative values and experiences involving ethics, aesthetics, and religion.[7] It has been further argued that some of our basic beliefs (belief in our existence, our awareness of each other and the world around us) may be justified or warranted even if not backed up by what people can produce as evidence.[8]

Whatever you think of this last claim, the idea that "evidence" is a clear and simple matter in philosophy is not itself universally evident. Some secular philosophers today are considered *anti-foundationalist* insofar as they reject the ideal of establishing a universally agreed-upon foundation for all legitimate claims of knowledge. The result need not be an *anything-goes anarchy*, but a realization that the (legitimate) reasons we have for some of our beliefs may be complicated, involving a cumulation of different experiences, shaped by culture and education. This can make the task of philosophy itself more complicated, but a massive amount of philosophical literature is evidence that there is still plenty of room for critical reflection, weighing the reasons that may warrant Christian faith or Buddhist teachings or making a case for secular atheism, radical skepticism, and so on.[9]

Reply to B. The few passages in the Bible that warn readers about philosophy may be interpreted as warnings about philosophies that are deeply hostile to

---

[7] I argue for this in multiple publications, beginning with *Consciousness and the Mind of God*. See also Goetz and Taliaferro (2008).

[8] This is a central claim in what is called Reformed Epistemology. Its leading advocate is Alvin Plantinga. For an accessible introduction, see his *Knowledge and Christian Belief*.

[9] See the four-volume *Encyclopedia of Philosophy of Religion* (Goetz and Taliaferro 2021).

Christian faith. Philosophies that relentlessly promote tyranny, vanity, and the love of personal or imperial glory may well be damaging to the virtues of humility, justice, mercy, and reverence for what is sacred, and may even be antithetical to the root meaning of "philosophy" itself. The term "philosophy" is derived from the Greek terms for "love" (*philo*) and wisdom (*sophia*) and is often translated as "the love of wisdom." It is hard to see that the worldviews of the Roman caesars in the first two centuries (think of Nero and Caligula) as celebrating the love of wisdom. On the other hand, the Bible contains many texts that extol the love of wisdom (including Ecclesiastes, Proverbs, the Wisdom of Solomon); in the New Testament, Paul is in a vibrant debate with philosophers (Acts 17, see especially verses 26–28), and many biblical passages have been used historically to promote the practice of philosophy by Christians (Psalm 19:1–6, Proverbs 5:6–11, Romans 1:19–20). There is reason to think that the Bible itself incorporates philosophy (the term *logos* in the Gospel of John is probably inspired by Platonic or Stoic sources). Some of the early Christians were identified as philosophers (Justin, Clement, Origen), and some of the first philosophers to publish in English were Christian philosophers (the Cambridge Platonists in the seventeenth century).

On the authority of the Bible, I have not (yet) observed an overt form of circular reasoning about the Bible being self-authenticating. The following exchange would be unhelpful:

Pat: The Bible is the Word of God.

Chris: How do you know that?

Pat: The Bible proclaims that it is the Word of God.

Chris: But how do you know that the Bible is reliable?

Pat: God would not lie or deceive.

Chris: I'll concede that if there is an all-good God, God would not lie or deceive, but how do you know that the Bible is the Word of God?

Pat: I know it is because the Bible proclaims that it is the Word of God.

Pat's reasoning is circular because Pat does not provide an independent reason for thinking that the Bible is the Word of God or reliable. Rather than such circular reasoning, it is common, historically and today, for a Christian to claim that the Bible is revelatory (or is the Word of God) on the basis of appealing to religious experience (many persons have testified that they have experienced God through the Bible; for a classic case, see Augustine's *Confessions*), historical evidence of the miraculous (the resurrection of Jesus Christ), or other forms of historical evidence (prophecies appear to be fulfilled or an argument that the development of the Christian tradition has a coherence and integrity that provides some evidence of providential guidance). Even if you find none of these reasons convincing, they at least do not have the circularity of asking you to believe the Bible on the grounds that "the Bible tells us so." That would be what Kant depicted as immature or abrogating the importance of courageously exercising your own intelligence. Alternatively, if exercising your own reason, you came to think the Bible was (or can function as) revelatory of the divine, it would seem as immature to reject it because of your freedom of intellect as it would be to reject the evidence available to you that some nonhuman animals can reveal their thoughts and emotions (perhaps through language or some other mode of communication) because of your freedom of intellect. I suggest that it seems to be an unhealthy bias to assume that, in principle, philosophers should reject all possible sources of divine revelation. At the same time, I suggest that it would be an unhealthy bias for "believers" in divine revelation (the Bible, the Quran, the Vedas, and more) to rule out, in principle, the evidential value of independent philosophical reflection.[10]

Pausing from the task of assessing whether Christian philosophy is a good or bad problem, let us take note of the variety of ways Christians view the Bible. The view of the Bible that is probably best known to Christians and their critics is the "conservative" position that the Bible is inerrant or free from error (at least in its original autographs/the original deposit of revelation). Inerrancy is usually held to be plenary – applying to the whole of the Bible – rather than, say, limited to matters of faith and morals but not (necessarily) in terms of historical accuracy (whether Jesus made only one journey to Jerusalem or multiple ones). Biblical inerrancy is sometimes defended on the grounds that a provident, omnipotent, all-good God would not allow errors in a revelation of God.

Seeing the Bible as revelation need not be a matter of reading the Bible "literally" insofar as it seems that significant biblical material can or should be read as metaphor or analogy. Most Christians historically and today have interpreted anthropomorphic language of God (references to God's hands and eyes) as metaphors. Some Christians treat the stories of Adam and Eve, Noah and the flood, Jonah and the fish, Job, and the conquest narratives of Joshua as parables. One may treat the Adamic (or Edenic) narrative as a parable, on the grounds of the evidence of evolution, while yet maintaining that the narrative

---

[10] The relationship between philosophy and claims of religious revelation is a huge topic in the history of ideas. For a history of this debate in modern, Western philosophy, see my book, *Evidence and Faith* (Taliaferro 2005). As I stated in footnote 1, I seek to avoid overly technical definitions in this Element, but I note here that for philosophies that take into account divine revelation, the boundary between what is labeled as "philosophy" and "theology" is fluid. For example, a new movement in the English-speaking world called "analytical theology" employs philosophical analytical tools in reflecting on theological claims. For those interested in definitions, see the second edition of *A Dictionary of Philosophy of Religion* coedited by myself and Elsa Marty.

sheds light on the nature of evildoing. Some Christians treat the conquest narratives in the book of Joshua as parables about overcoming evil or as Middle Eastern hyperbole rather than as historical events on ethical grounds, based on the conviction that the God of love would not command what today would be called genocide. On the other hand, there are philosophers committed to inerrancy who affirm an original creation of humans and who defend the ethical propriety of the conquest narratives.

Because the conservative view of the Bible is such a huge target for critics, three further factors are good to bear in mind: treating the Bible as inerrant revelation can allow for phenomenology; for example, in Joshua 10:13, perhaps the sun *appeared to stand still*, which is different from the claim that it actually did stand still (or Earth ceased to rotate). Second, inerrancy does not entail that all that is recorded as done by biblical patriarchs (Abraham's deception in Genesis 20) is good. Third, advocating biblical inerrancy is not the same as claiming that God dictated the contents of the Bible to human authors. Inerrancy is only the view that the extant Bible (or its original form) is free from error. It does not preclude the view that one of the sources for the composition of the Bible is human, creative imagination.

Not all Christians adopt a "conservative" view of the Bible. A different position is taken by many Christians who hold that the Bible is *about revelation* and *it can become a vehicle for revelation*. Some theologians contend that Jesus Christ is the revelation of God and, ideally, the New Testament functions as a portal or means by which we may encounter the person of Jesus Christ, perhaps as testified to by the working of the Holy Spirit (the *Testimonium Interim Spiritu Sanctu*; Hebrews 10:15; 1 John 5:7–8). Hans Urs von Balthasar advocates this view of revelation when he explicitly denies that the Bible is the word of God: "Although ever since the time of Luther we have become accustomed to call the Bible 'God's Word,' it is not Sacred Scripture which is God's original language and self-expression, but rather Jesus Christ" (Balthasar 1982, 29).

This view of the Bible and revelation is customarily articulated in terms of *the Bible being inspired but not inerrant*. On this view, we may not have the exact words of Christ (the *ipsissima verba*) in each of the four gospels, but in reflecting on all four gospels we can hear the voice of Christ (the *ipsissima vox*). On this view, the Bible becomes not an end in itself (the *objectum quod*) but that through which we encounter the object of faith (the *objectum quo*), the triune God. From the standpoint of this model of revelation, the Old Testament is a *record of events and acts* (experiences of the divine through covenants, acts of faith, the exodus out of Egypt, prophecies, reported visions and dreams, the praise and lessons of the Psalms and wisdom literature) that we may come to experience as revelations of God.

This view is sometimes misleadingly described as a nonpropositional account of revelation. It is misleading insofar as it is difficult for Christians to refer to revelation without relying on propositional statements (God appeared to Moses through a burning bush), but the point at issue is that (on this second view exemplified by the Catholic von Balthasar and the Protestant Karl Barth) the revelation itself is mediated by the Bible as a sacred text, as opposed to the revelation being the very same thing as the propositional statements in the Bible. So, in reply to the second source of suspicion about Christian philosophers and the Bible, rarely is the Bible advanced as self-authenticating (using circular reasoning), the Bible has multiple passages, and whole books, promoting philosophy as a practice, and one needs to appreciate that not all Christians adopt the conservative view of biblical inerrancy.

The less conservative treatment of the Bible has allowed many Christian philosophers and theologians to adopt what is often called *progressive revelation*. On this view, some of the New Testament elements that now seem culturally alien to many – the permissive acceptance of slavery, Pauline teaching that women should be silent in church, the view that homosexuality is wrong – have been seen by some Christians as faults that the church needs to correct. In some Christian communities today, these have in fact been abrogated in light of what is believed to be "Jesus's way of love" (contemporary, popular Anglican phrase to stress the openness of the church to LGBTQIA persons).

Reply to C. First observation: Russell's criticism of Aquinas is not based on any examples he offers of when Aquinas seems to abandon a philosophical argument because it undermines Catholic faith, nor is it based on Russell's psychoanalytic study of Aquinas's character, drives, motives, and the like. So let's put to one side Russell's focus on Aquinas himself and consider the general point at issue. Maybe Russell's point is that a true philosopher should not know (or claim to know or believe) the answers to philosophical questions (like "Does God exist?" "Is there free will?" "Does life have meaning?" "Are there moral truths like killing the innocent is wrong?" "Do I exist?" "Might everything I believe I see be a mere dream or illusion?") prior to engaging in philosophy.

If that criterion for genuine philosophy was adopted, it would rule out a great deal of what the world recognizes as bona fide philosophical work. Many philosophers, historically and today, seem to embark in philosophy guided by their pre-philosophical convictions. In the tradition of commonsense philosophy from Thomas Reid in the eighteenth century to G. E. Moore and Roderick Chisholm in the twentieth, many philosophers, perhaps going back even to Plato and Aristotle, have assumed (seemingly prior to philosophical argument) that persons exist and endure over time, that we perceive each other, that we have bodies, emotions, desires, reason, 2+2=4, and so on. Surely they cannot be ruled out as true philosophers (lovers of wisdom) for having such pre-philosophical convictions. Actually, some secular philosophers such as David Hume are so committed to some pre-philosophical beliefs and practices that they do not abandon them in the wake of what they concede are powerful skeptical objections. Famously, Hume commends persisting to believe in induction (and that the future will resemble the past) even if one cannot defend such a belief by reason without begging the question.

Revising Russell's claim, perhaps we should think that a skillful philosopher might well start off with a belief or judgment on a philosophical matter but then be willing to engage in self-criticism, asking whether their initial beliefs and judgments (claims, intuitions) are indeed true or justified. Do we have compelling reasons to think that Christians who practice philosophy never consider whether Christian faith might be false or unjustified? No. As autobiographies of philosophers proliferate, we seem to have abundant cases of Christians rejecting Christianity in the course of practicing philosophy (Russell gave up his religious convictions in so doing); lots of non-Christians have claimed to come to Christianity through philosophy (H. D. Lewis), and the same kinds of shifts have been recorded by persons being led to different religions via philosophy as well as led to abandon or shift religions.[11]

I suggest that the enduring positive point behind Russell's objection is that it is desirable for philosophers to guard against the love of wisdom being marred by a host of factors, including fear of philosophical challenges, lack of imagination, refusal to consider worldviews radically different from one's own, bias, tribalism, vanity, threats of ostracism or persecution from the church or state or family, and so on. With that in mind, I suggest there is nothing inherently wrong with beginning philosophy as a Christian or Buddhist or secular atheist, so long as one is willing to engage in critical reflection on one's initial beliefs, consider other alternatives, and the like. The revised, Russell-inspired objection to Christian philosophy is especially ineffective as the term "Christian philosophy" is being used in this Element, as it is recognized that non-Christians (such as self-described "friendly atheist" William Rowe) have contributed to Christian philosophy. None of those philosophers can be accused of being unphilosophical because of their prior Christian convictions.

1.3 Some Warning Labels about God and Christian Philosophy

Notwithstanding the defense of the integrity of Christian philosophy, I suggest that at least two, related warning labels may be appropriate. First, though not at all impossible, it *can be difficult* for Christians to step back from their Christian

---

[11] See *God and the Philosophers* (Morris 1996) and *Philosophers without Gods* (Antony 2010).

commitment to assess the philosophical merits of Christian faith. I will qualify this worry later in this Element. A second worry for Christians is that the boundary between philosophy and apologetics can become blurred. Again, I will qualify this worry. Both warnings stem from the fact that Christianity is a comprehensive way of life in which devotion, faith, love, and other values are prized. While in this Element I propose that non-Christians contribute to Christian philosophy, I am now addressing when observant Christians practice philosophy. These are the people Alvin Plantinga addressed in a famous 1984 essay, "Advice to Christian Philosophers," which concludes with this paragraph: "In sum, we who are Christians and propose to be philosophers must not rest content with being philosophers who happen, incidentally to be Christians; we must strive to be Christian philosophers. We must therefore pursue our projects with integrity, independence, and Christian boldness" (Plantinga 1984, 271). Let's focus on the comprehensiveness of Christianity and then consider the two warnings.

Christianity is not just a philosophy (in the sense of being a worldview and values), but a way of life. According to tradition, Christians are called to love God and neighbor, to seek justice, to practice compassion, to go to the aid of the vulnerable (following the example of the Good Samaritan), and to join other Christians in communities of worship, love of God and neighbor, prayer, confession, and repentance. There are sacramental rites of initiation (baptism), rites for regular, sustained life (the Eucharist – sometimes called Mass, Communion, or the Lord's Supper), ordinations to religious orders, marriage rites, last rites, and funerals. Moreover, monks and nuns commit to regular times of prayer, including the recitation of 150 psalms. There are retreats, pilgrimages, meditations, fasting and feasting, house blessings, vigils, inspiring artwork, architecture, music, poetry, and films.

These traditions and rites need not handicap a Christian in the practice of philosophy in any way. But mainstream philosophy is often practiced in religiously neutral or secular conditions shorn of a religious ethos – dialogues and lectures, college and university classrooms and seminars, conferences, journals, books, coffeehouses, museums, novels, and poetry, in addition to emails, text messages, and podcasts. There are occasional academic ceremonies with robes, artwork, and music. There are even philosophical tattoos! Recent years have brought renewed interest in how philosophy itself counts as a way of life that has a spiritual dimension.[12]

Still, philosophy as practiced in most philosophical institutions throughout the world today is not the systematic structure we see in Christian religious

---

[12] See Pierre Hadot's *Philosophy As a Way of Life* (Hadot 1995).

practice, and keeping the spheres of religion and mainstream philosophy distinct can be important. For example, several Christian philosophers were elected as presidents of the largest, all-inclusive professional philosophical associations in the United States. What if one of them, in their presidential address to the American Philosophical Association, started giving a sermon or singing a hymn?![13]

More seriously, consider how it can be a strain for practicing Christians to detach and earnestly seek to critically evaluate their faith. Christian philosopher Richard Creel asks the following question: "If you were given an opportunity to choose between (1) knowing the way reality is and (2) having enduring faith that there is a God in the classical theistic sense, on the condition that you could not have both and your choice would be irreversible, which would you choose?" (Creel 1984, 230).

Creel begins by supposing that we should choose the first, but then questions how important knowledge is versus the goods enabled by faith. Knowing some realities (how many grains of sand are on a beach) seems pointless whereas having faith in God can be life-enhancing and provide grounds to believe that, no matter what tragedies befall us, there is hope for universal happiness.

> Speaking abstractly, it seems to me that my highest moral obligation is to believe and live in a way that is compatible with and supportive of the supreme value; the supreme value, I believe, is universal happiness. This entails that I should hold beliefs, or at least have hopes, that are compatible with and supportive of this possibility. Now certainly the achievement of universal happiness is possible in some significant sense if there is a God. It may or may not be possible if there is not a God. If there is not a God and therefore universal happiness may not be possible, I would rather not know it; I would rather have faith that there is such a being and that therefore universal happiness is possible. My highest moral obligation, then, is not to seek knowledge but to honor the good. Should someone try to take away my faith in the reality of the good by attempting to persuade me that the truth about reality is such that we cannot rejoice in it, I would and should resist with all my resources. If my own mind begins to assault me with doubts in addition to difficulties, I should belittle its powers. (Creel 1984, 231)

Creel has crafted a fascinating thought experiment, though two things should be kept in mind, First, enduring faith in God's goodness and power seems to require that "believers" think that the reality is that there truly is a good, powerful God. To go back to a point made earlier in this section, to believe

---

[13] I jest; there is zero percent chance this would occur, but on occasion, Christian religious services are held at philosophy conferences hosted by the SCP.

there is a God is not to believe something you know is false. Faith in God requires belief, or at least the hope that there truly is a God.

Second, the whole idea of someone being given Creel's original choice seems strange. Perhaps paradoxically, I am tempted to think that being given the option "to know the way reality is" might require having the option to become omniscient or to have an omniscient (hence godlike) guide. Be that as it may, Creel does raise a point worth weighing: if you are a Christian and your faith is deeply bound up in your commitment to the well-being of others, and the loss of that faith will likely lead to despair, will you be highly motivated to expunge that faith through philosophical criticism?

Anticipating some objections, I am not endorsing a pragmatic case for philosophical or religious beliefs. A false belief might confer great benefits. Impressive data support the hypothesis that, at least in the United States, some religious practice leads to longer life, less depression, less suicide, less substance abuse and divorce, a greater report of satisfaction or happiness, and so on, compared with those who do not have some religious practice (see Taliaferro 2021). While not evidence of the veracity of the religious beliefs underlying such practices, these factors may lead practitioners to be reluctant to engage in robust detachment and getting enthusiastic about philosophical critiques of Christianity (constant rereading by Christian philosophers of new atheist literature, memorizing the critique of Christianity by Nietzsche, Feuerbach, Freud, et al.).

Traditionally, the relationship between God and the soul has been likened to the intimacy of a marriage (Hosea, Song of Songs, the sermons of St. Bernard of Clairvaux), which can make a quest to end what one takes to be a relationship with God the equivalent of a quest for the breakup and divorce of an intimate marriage. Christian philosophical tradition has included bold figures like Søren Kierkegaard who call self-identified Christians to radically call into question their faith. And yet there is this admonition in the Epistle of James about how to petition God prayerfully: "But let him ask [God] in faith without doubting, for the one who doubts is like the surf of the sea driven and tossed by the wind" (James 1:6).[14]

A second worry: occasions arise when it is important for Christian philosophers to distinguish philosophy from apologetics. This is a controversial matter, partly because of disagreement about the definition of "apologetics."

"Apologetics" is defined in multiple ways today, but in this context, I am using it to refer to the practice of seeking to convert persons to the Christian

---

[14] For a virtual textbook of cases when devout, even passionate Christian prayers can blend belief and doubt, see *The Harper Collins Book of Prayers*. I particularly recommend a study of prayers by Kierkegaard, 228–230.

faith, often through reasoned argument. I do not at all suggest that the advocacy of Christian faith through philosophy is always bad. In fact, I have deep admiration for good Christian apologetics and some of my own writing, such as my book *The Golden Cord*, could be classified as a case of apologetics (Taliaferro 2012). I did not write that book with an explicit desire to convert my readers to Christianity, but I do make a philosophical case in it for Christianity, and it would not make me dejected to learn that a reader was led to Christian faith or at least led to think of it as an option.

Still, there are public forums, classrooms and seminars in secular universities and colleges, international philosophy conferences, and so on, where philosophy is practiced in inclusive, diverse ways and where Christian apologetics would seem out of place. I make this suggestion hesitantly, as many secular philosophers may be understood as seeking to persuade, even convert others. For example, it is not unfair to see secular atheist Peter Singer as wanting to persuade others to become vegans, to contribute more to famine relief, and so on. In a generic sense, Singer seems to be akin to Christian apologists (like William Craig). Some philosophers today seem to be unlike Singer (a philosophy friend has told me that when he argues for atheism at conferences and in journals, he is not seeking to persuade anyone to become an atheist; he is simply engaging others in inquiry).

When I am practicing philosophy in my college's classrooms or at the American Philosophical Association, I am careful to focus on the practice of philosophy itself, and not to think for a second about the topic of conversion. During office hours, if a student or colleague asks me why they might consider Christian faith, I am prepared to share what I believe to be relevant, good philosophical reasons, but this is not something I would make part of a course.

I think we do well to recognize that the distinction between philosophy and apologetics is not always clear.[15] Even so, matters of religious conversion are more appropriately addressed in settings that are explicitly identified as sites for apologetics.[16] Overall, it is good for philosophical forums to exist that are dedicated to open, free exchanges. In such forums, Christian students may argue for the cogency of Buddhism, secular atheists might contend that Hinduism is more convincing than Marxism, religious practitioners might express their doubts, and New Atheists could talk about their spiritual longing.

---

[15] An interesting case of the lack of a clear distinction is C. S. Lewis. Today, he is often described as a Christian apologist, but increasingly entries on Lewis in philosophical encyclopedias describe him as a philosopher. For an overview on apologetics, see *The History of Apologetics*, which includes a chapter on Lewis (Forrest, Chatraw, and McGrath 2002). I contributed a chapter, "William Paley Apologetics for Design and Culture" (344–354).

[16] See "Testimony, Evidence and Wisdom in Today's Philosophy of Religion" (Taliaferro and Duel 2011).

Maybe in a Russellian spirit but adding a twist, I suggest that it is good to have philosophical forums where persons are encouraged to question their own convictions, to use imaginative sympathy to understand alternatives, and to do so without fear of ostracism or other ills. Setting up such forums is different from setting up a site to convert those present to Christianity or some other religion, or to inculcate exclusively secular values.[17] I add a minor note that the motivation of Christians to bring more persons to faith can vary widely: it may be due to a love of God and neighbor and a desire to share that love, to a desire to save others from divine judgment, or from yet other motives.[18]

2 Is God's Transcendence a Problem for Christian Philosophy?

Does God speak? Does God have a mouth? Hands? Eyes? The Bible is replete with such language. The Bible refers to God's speaking from the beginning (Genesis 1), and images abound of God walking and talking with prophets. God is pictured or described as an animal: a lion, a lamb, an eagle, even a mother hen. And from the standpoint of the orthodox belief that Jesus is fully human and fully divine, God-incarnate was conceived and born, grew from childhood to adulthood, ate, drank, taught, listened, performed acts of healing and other miracles, slept, and was arrested, put on trial, tortured, and executed. He died and after three days was resurrected, appearing to many, and then ascended to God the Father.

Historically and today, Christian philosophers have wrestled with language about God, treating some terms as metaphors (God is like a lion), and others literally or univocally – Jesus truly suffered, and not just metaphorically. Christian philosophers have done much work to contrast God and the created order. By their lights, we are plagued by ignorance, while God is all-knowing or omniscient; we are highly limited in power, while God is all-powerful or omnipotent; we are prone to vice and wrongdoing, while God is essentially good; we have finite material bodies, while God is incorporeal and not limited to a finite, spatial body or location (the exception being the incarnate Jesus Christ); we have a beginning in time, while God has no beginning in time; we are perishable, vulnerable to premature violent death,

---

[17] See "Is Strategic Thinking Desirable in Philosophical Reflection?" (Taliaferro and Churchill 2015).

[18] A thought experiment may be fitting: if you thought a bomb was planted at a philosophy conference, wouldn't you zealously try to rescue your colleagues? Some traditional Christians think that a rejection of the lordship of Christ may lead to a fate even more terrible than dying due to a bomb. Beliefs about life after death and the atonement can deeply impact the desire to bring persons to religious faith. It may also be noted that the zeal of secularists to spread secularism can be deeply impacted by the belief that religions are dangerous.

whereas God is the indestructible and imperishable creator and sustainer of the cosmos, albeit in the incarnation, Jesus was vulnerable and suffered a premature, violent death.

In regard to God's relation to the cosmos, most Christians hold that the cosmos is contingent; it is the result of a free creation of God who sustains its existence over time. God is not contingent. God was not created by a higher, more powerful God, or by a law of nature, or by chance. God did not create God (being self-caused or *causa sui*), but unlike us, who can desire to cease to be, God affirms God's own being and is said to be self-existing or existing necessarily (*ens necessarium*).

Some Christian philosophers rely heavily, even exclusively, on the Bible to identify divine attributes, while others combine the Bible with philosophical reflection on God as a maximally (unsurpassably) excellent being. In what is known as *perfect being theology*, God is greater than which cannot be conceived. The divine attributes that Christian philosophers debate include God's relationship to time (some hold that God is timeless and created time, others that God is temporal but without temporal beginning or end), whether God is immutable or changing, impassable (subject to emotions), or simple (sometimes understood as God's attributes all being one). I postpone to Section 4 reflection on the Trinity.

What has been sketched so far is enough to consider what may be a problem for Christian philosophy. How can we reconcile all of this thinking and speaking about God when the Bible itself seems to affirm that God is beyond our thoughts and inscrutable? "For my thoughts are not your thoughts, nor are your ways my ways, says the Lord. For as the heavens are higher than the earth, so are my ways higher than your ways and my thoughts than your thoughts" (Isaiah 55:8–9). "O the depth of the riches and wisdom and knowledge of God! How unsearchable are his judgments and how inscrutable his ways!" (Romans 11:33–34).

That God is ineffable and beyond the power of human cognition is affirmed in Christian tradition. Consider this passage from sixth-century theologian Pseudo-Dionysius: "The inscrutable One is out of the reach of every rational process. Nor can any words come up to the inexpressible Good, this One, this Source of all unity, this supra-existence Being. Mind beyond mind, word beyond speech, it is gathered up by no discourse, by no intuition, by no name" (Pseudo-Dionysius 1987, 50).

The Cloud of Unknowing, a fourteenth-century Christian classic by an anonymous English mystic, is in agreement when it says that all thoughts and concepts of God should be buried beneath a "cloud of forgetting" while our love of God should rise up into a "cloud of unknowing." Theology that stresses the unknowability of God is often referred to as *apophatic (negative) theology*. Let us first consider God's transcendence as a problem.

2.1 God Is a Problem because God Is beyond Space and Time, Human Language and Concepts

There are at least three areas to consider: (A) We are in a world of space and time, whereas God is believed to be beyond space and time. (B) God is utterly unique and thus beyond description. (C) The very idea of analyzing the concept of God is religiously suspect as it can be a way of seeking to control God or to diminish God, treating God like a thing.

(A) The reality of space and time seems indisputable. It is obvious that we live in a world of objects and events spread out spatially and temporally. We know that the same spatial object (your cup of coffee) cannot fully occupy two separate places or spatial regions at the same time, whereas different spatial objects can be in the same space at different times. Time is one-directional (past-present-and future is not reversible so that the future must come after the past and present), whereas space is not (spatial objects can move about in space). Our communication and language for and about each other and our world reflects our spatiotemporal reality. To speak of a divine reality beyond space and time is absurd, or at least beyond our linguistic and cognitive powers.

(B) Reflecting on and speaking of God is problematic because of God's uniqueness. Our description of one another and the things around us often involve comparisons and contrasts. But God is incomparably unique. Hugh McCabe stresses the uniqueness of God as *sui generis* as opposed to being one of a kind.

> God must be incomprehensible to us precisely because he is creator of all that is and, as Aquinas puts it, outside the order of all beings. God therefore cannot be classified as any kind of being. God cannot be compared to or contrasted with other things in respect of what they are like as dogs can be compared and contrasted with cats and both of them with stones or stars. God is not an inhabitant of the universe; he is the reason why there is a universe at all. God is in everything holding it constantly in existence but he is not located anywhere, nor is what it is to be God located anywhere in logical space. When you have finished classifying and counting all the things in the universe you cannot add: "And also there is God." When you have finished classifying and counting everything in the universe you have finished, period. There is no God in the world. (McCabe 2002, 37)

By McCabe's lights the very concept of God prevents us from thinking or speaking of God as one being among others.

D. Z. Phillips offers this intriguing case for not thinking of God as some kind of thing, like a unicorn or a planet:

> If there is an analogy between the existence of God and the existence of unicorns, then coming to see that there is a God would be like coming to see that an additional being exists. "I know what people are doing when they worship," a philosopher might say. "They praise, they confess, they thank, and they ask for things. The only difference between myself and religious believers is that I do not believe that there is a being who receives their worship." The assumption, here, is that the meaning of worship is contingently related to the question whether there is a God or not. The assumption might be justified by saying that there need be no consequences of existential beliefs. Just as one can say, "There is a planet, but I couldn't care less." ... But all this is foreign to the question of whether there is a God. That is not something anyone can *find out*. It has been far too readily assumed that the dispute between the believer and the unbeliever is over *a matter of fact*. (Phillips 1970, 16–17)

If Phillips is right, then we should not think of God as a thing, even an extraordinary, awesome thing, that as a matter of fact exists or does not exist.

(C) Another worry about forming concepts of God and all their analytical distinctions is whether this can be a way of domesticating or controlling God. Perhaps the most fitting response to a truly transcendent being should be reverential silence. Martin Buber, a great twentieth-century Jewish philosopher, might provide a fitting warning to Christian philosophers. According to Buber, there are personal relations he referred to using the terms I-Thou as opposed to our relationship to things (I-It relations). In the spirit of Buber, one may well wonder: does the analytical philosophical conceptualization of God turn God into a thing, an "It"? Does this pit Christian philosophy at odds with a deeply Christian spirituality?

2.2 But What if God Is Both Transcendent and Immanent, Present and Omnipresent?

Before responding to these three worries, I offer two paragraphs with some technical distinctions.

When it comes to language used about the divine, philosophers often distinguish between the literal (or univocal), the analogical, and the equivocal. So it seems to be literal when the word "knowledge" is used in saying "God knows your thoughts" and "You know what you are thinking." The same general meaning of "knowledge" may be in play even if the way God knows your thoughts is (presumably) very different from the way you do. In Latin, this distinction is sometimes made by using the term *res significata* when referring to what is predicated of, say, God and a human when it is claimed that "God knows what you know," and the term *modus significandi* is sometimes used when referring to the modes of what is predicated, as in "how God knows reality is different from how we know reality." Analogical language involves presumed similarities between referents. So the expression "Alex is a prince among men" is analogical insofar as Alex is thought of as deserving our respect and attention. Language is used equivocally when the term has two meanings, as in the use of the word "bark": "Look at the bark on the tree" and "I thought the dog would bark when it saw that rodent."

Relatedly, it is also important to note the distinction between symbols and pictures. In some religious traditions, images and concepts used of God or the divine are often meant to be symbols rather than pictorial representations. It is amazing how often this is lost on both theoreticians and practitioners of religion. In the Bible, as we have seen at the outset of this section, God is sometimes described in anthropomorphic terms. Thus, Psalm 34:15 says that "The eyes of the Lord are on the righteous, and his ears are attentive to his cry." And Psalm 119:73 says this, in reference to God's creation of the Psalmist: "Your hands made me and formed me." It would be a mistake to take these images as pictures of God, thus viewing God as a humanlike being with literal eyes and ears and hands. Rather, they are meant to be symbols referring to the care and attentiveness of the Creator toward the creation. Now, on to replying to the three objections.

One response to all three objections would be for Christian philosophers to propose that all their work on divine attributes should be taken as symbols or metaphors, or in highly analogical terms. Often the sign of a metaphor is that it is false, if used literally, as in "Juliet is the sun" (it is false that Juliet is a gaseous blob with 10,000-degree heat and a diameter of more than 430,000 miles). *God has eyes that roam around the earth* is literally false and thus likely a metaphorical attribution.

Another response is to challenge each of the objections, claiming that they are based on a truncated view of thought and language, a misunderstanding of God's uniqueness, and a suspect notion of control, concepts, and what it is to be a thing (an object or substance).

Reply to A. Are our language and thought essentially spatial? It seems not: the truth of mathematical propositions (2+2=4) do not have a size or location, nor do the laws of logic (A is A, or everything is itself or self-identical). Even thoughts (*The term "Christian philosophy" does not appear in most philosophy dictionaries*) do not have a certain weight, color, volume, or spatial location. In Christianity, God is not identified with a spatial object, but God is understood to be *omnipresent*; there is no place where God is not. God is everywhere. So referring to God is not a matter of referring to some absent, finite spirit, a very powerful poltergeist in a haunted house or planet or specific galaxy. Before turning to the language of God and time, I offer a brief, further observation about divine omnipresence.

A classic, Christian account of God's omnipresence is in terms of God's power and knowledge. To claim that God is present where you are reading this Element (a coffeehouse, let's say) is to claim that the coffeehouse is sustained in its existence by God's creative power (it would cease to be if God were to withdraw this sustaining power), that God knows all truths about where you are and all those present, and that God can act directly on that region of space, levitating your coffee mug and the like. God's action, as well as God's knowledge, are direct insofar as they are not mediated by bodily organs or physical mechanisms.

In my view, there is a further dimension to God's presence that is found in the Bible and in Christian experience to the effect that God is affectively responsive to the values and disvalues of each place. This is controversial for it amounts to claiming that God is not impassable (not subject to emotions), but the Christian vision of God includes what appears to be God's delight, love, and anger. If you are in the coffeehouse plotting some racist cruelty, it is difficult to imagine that the God revealed by Jesus Christ is aloof and indifferent. You, or at least your plotting, are fittingly thought of as subject to God's angry hatred, just as you are the object of God's love if you are in the coffeehouse confessing some sin in the course of reconciling with your sibling whom you wronged ten years ago.

Language, time, and God. As far as our language and thought being restricted to temporal events, it should be borne in mind that all thought and language must transcend time insofar as it is not confined to the instant. An instant in time is, strictly speaking, of no duration at all. We cannot think or speak or do anything in an instant. An instant in time is like a point in space; it takes up no volume. An instant is, as it were, shorter than the shortest measure of time we have. The shortest measurement of time we have now is the time it takes a light particle to cross a hydrogen molecule – 242 zeptoseconds (a trillionth of a billionth of a second) – but that is still an interval rather than an instant. We live in events, in intervals between instants, but not in an instant.

An initial reply to an objection about divine transcendence is therefore that there is a sense in which *all of us transcend time in terms of instants*. We also seem capable of understanding truths that seem timeless. The truth of 2+2=4 is not temporally locatable – for example, it is true at midnight on the world clock. There is also what is sometimes called the logical use of the predicate "to be" (or is). The truth of the statement "Socrates is wise" is sometimes interpreted as Socrates was wise, is wise, or will be wise. Statements like "Unicorns are single horned" might also be atemporal (sadly, there are no unicorns, but, if there were one, it would be single horned). Moreover, as just suggested, you yourself transcend time insofar as you must live beyond temporal instants.

Stepping back, there are at least three alternatives to consider in addressing the problem of God transcending time. The first is to claim that the God of Christianity is temporal. God is without temporal beginning or end, but there is a past, present, and future for God. This view is favored especially by those who give primacy to the biblical portrait of God. There at least appears to be a temporal sequence to the acts of God who appears to Abraham and Sarah, then to Moses, and so on. God is not subject to terrestrial time or atomic clocks, but God's existential now is in accord with the now or present of creatures. God hears your prayers as God (at the same time) hears the prayers of extraterrestrials in distant galaxies. This view is sometimes referred to as *open theism*, according to which the future is genuinely open for God and free creatures. There is more than one possible future and free agents can shape its direction. Christian philosophers who contend that God transcends time (God is timelessly eternal) hold that God hears your payers on, say, Thursday, but God timelessly knows of your prayer without being subject to temporal sequences.

A second alternative is to adopt some form of four-dimensionalism. On this view, the notion of what for us is past, present, and future is largely subjective. Time is real, but events may be described using terms like *prior to*, *simultaneous with*, and *subsequent to* rather than using the terms *past*, *present*, and *future*. This reframing of our reference to events allows us to refer to events in history from a timeless or tenseless point of view. *You are reading this text now* would become *you are reading this text in 2925*. This position has some following in contemporary physics. On this view, God may be revealed in sequence, but these appearances are timelessly, nonsequentially willed. God timelessly wills that God be revealed on Mt. Sinai to Moses and later revealed as Jesus in Palestine. God thus timelessly wills that God be revealed in time. This is the classical view of God and time defended by many Christian philosophers, historically and today.

A third option is some kind of hybrid of the first two. It has been argued that God was timelessly eternal prior to God creating time. But once God creates time, God enters it. This may sound odd because it entails that there was no time before God created time. So, if God created on what we call Monday, there was no prior duration, no Sunday. This view has the support of some traditional Christian philosophers who depict the Incarnation as the eternal, timeless God entering time as Jesus of Nazareth.

Reply to B. I suggest that the uniqueness of God is no barrier to reflection and language about God. Despite McCabe being a Dominican priest, in the same religious order in the Roman Catholic Church as Thomas Aquinas, he seems to bypass much Christian theology (and biblical language) when he claims that it is illicit to compare and contrast God and creation or creatures. We (and our dogs, to use McCabe's example) are contingent and are ignorant of many things, whereas (if God exists) God is noncontingent (a necessary being) and omniscient. According to tradition, God is in the world, omnipresent, dwelling everywhere. If you counted (in the sense of taking into account) all of reality, presumably a theist would add something like *There is an omnipresent, necessarily existing creator and sustainer of the cosmos*. And the atheist would deny that reality includes God. As for God not being "a being" or a thing, see the next reply.

In response to Phillips's amusing observation about how language of God differs from language about unicorns and planets, I suggest that it does not support his claim that the existence of God is not a matter of facts. Unicorns and planets are profoundly different from God (if there is a God); unicorns and planets are contingent, finite beings as opposed to being candidates for necessarily existing and being omnipresent, the creator and sustainer of the cosmos. Moreover, his claim that God's existence cannot be a matter of fact is puzzling because it would then make sense to claim that "There is a God, but I couldn't care less." We can imagine persons believing all kinds of what they take to be matters of fact but then treating with detachment (e.g., they believe that their biological death means their permanent nonexistence). Perhaps Phillips's point would be plausible if by "God" one means "a Being that all persons care about." It would be at least odd to claim "There is a Being that all persons care about but I do not care about." Without some such stipulation, it seems that theists and nontheists can refer to God with varying levels of belief, disbelief, passionate care, or aloof indifference.

Reply to C. Granted, sometimes our concepts and language about ourselves, others, even God, can be used to manipulate and exploit. And, sadly, most of us know the problems that arise from falling in love with the concept (picture or image) of another person that turns out to be false or misleading. And presumably, most of us know the ill effects of being treated as a mere thing as opposed to a person. Martin Buber was masterful in exposing the danger of ideologies that diminish the integrity and dignity of being a person. Granting all of this, two elements need to be considered: loving God or anyone or anything requires some concept of God or the object of one's love. And terms like "thing" or "being" may be used of human beings and God without overshadowing matters of dignity, worth, and vital, even overwhelming importance.

On the first element, imagine claiming to love something referred to as X, while claiming to not have any idea or any concept of X whatever. Imagine that any proposed description of X (using language that is literal, analogical, metaphorical, or symbolic) is deemed unworthy and of zero credibility or assistance. Eventually, I believe, most of us would conclude that the claim to love X is nonsensical (perhaps a joke). Communication with others about X would be pointless and the idea of having a community devoted to X would be absurd without some descriptive concept of X. An appeal might also be made to the meaningfulness of atheism and agnosticism. Arguably, when atheists deny the existence of God and agnostics claim not to know whether God exists, their claims would have little meaning unless it is granted that some concept (or descriptive content) of "God" is licit (appropriate, intelligible).

On the second element, philosophers sometimes use the term "thing" broadly to refer to events, processes, relations, properties, propositions, and numbers and not just to concrete individual things. In this broad usage – and you judge it inappropriate to refer to God as a thing – it appears you are claiming God is nothing (a term that is short for no-thing). If you intend to claim *there is no God* (or *atheism is true*), there is no problem. But to claim that God is (or God may be worshipped or prayed to) and yet God is nothing is a problem.

On a broader point, those who go so far as to doubt the very existence of things or objects or substances (terms that can be used interchangeably) face a problem of incoherence; to engage in doubt, you have to be a doubter (a thing or substance that doubts). So, in reply to McCabe, I suggest that, if there is a God, God is not nothing or no-thing, but the transcendent, omnipresent Creator and sustainer of the creation, a reality that lovingly pervades the cosmos with unsurpassable goodness and power.

Going back to the beginning of this section, what are we to make of the passage from Isaiah: "For my thoughts are not your thoughts, nor are your ways my ways, says the Lord. For as the heavens are higher than the earth, so are my ways higher than your ways and my thoughts than your thoughts"? I suggest that this passage would make no sense unless it makes sense to believe that God has thoughts. To say that our thoughts are not God's may be a way of claiming that God's thoughts are distinct from ours, not subject to our control. To claim that God's thoughts are higher than ours is (contra McCabe) a comparison. What of the lines from Romans: "O the depth of the riches and wisdom and knowledge of God! How unsearchable are his judgments and how inscrutable his ways!"? Again, there is a hint of comparison (God's wisdom and knowledge are deeper than our wisdom and knowledge). To claim that God's judgments are unsearchable and inscrutable cannot mean they are completely unknowable or unconceivable, for how might we refer to God's judgments unless we have some notion that God makes judgments, and perhaps too have some notion of a divine judgment? As for Pseudo-Dionysius and *The Cloud of Unknowing*, perhaps these are dramatic claims that God is much more than our thoughts, concepts, languag – which is different than claiming that God is like X (utterly and completely opaque) in the earlier thought experiment.

2.3 Minding the Remoteness and Nearness of God

There are at least two elements about the remoteness and nearness of God for Christian philosophers to address: the hiddenness of God and the idea that God may be present to creatures in an interior sense. Can we make sense of St. Augustine when he addresses God and proclaims, "You were more inward to me than my most inward part," or, as it is sometimes paraphrased, "you were closer to me than I am to myself" (Book 3 of *Confessions*)? (The Latin is *tu autem eras interior intimo meo.*)

Divine hiddenness. Some argue that if the God of Christianity exists, God would not be remotely transcendent, but more apparent and immanent, especially to those seeking to know whether God exists and to live in his presence (*Coram Deo*). If a relationship with God is so fruitful and beneficial, and God loves creatures, why isn't God's loving presence more generously evident? Even for practicing Christians there can be periods of aridity when God feels absent (*Deus adsconditus*) or retired (*Deus emeritus*), a period sometimes referred to as the dark night of the soul.

In reply, some Christian philosophers claim that God is more apparent than critics suppose. A person (a human person or divine) may be apparent or revealed when others do not recognize such appearances or revelations. Perhaps the Bible is a vehicle that genuinely is revelatory even when skeptical readers deny it. I might make a public revelation of some kind (confessing that I have a Plato tattoo), and it is no less of a revelation even if no one believes it.

Undoubtedly, an objector will persist: surely the God of Christianity who is supposed to love the world would be more *evidently* and *cogently* revealed. So, even if the Bible and Christian tradition are revelatory (they accurately depict the presence of God), what good is that if the revelation is not made compelling, both for skeptics and for persons of faith enduring a sense of God's absence?

In reply it has been claimed that at some point the God of Christianity will indeed be compellingly revealed to all persons (Luke 3:6), but in this life God's not being overwhelmingly obvious may be essential for human freedom and for some virtues. If it was obvious that there is an omnipotent God of justice, and you knew justice will be meticulously administered (either in this life or the next), you might pursue justice only out of prudence, a desire to avoid being punished or a desire for some future felicity. If you do not know there is a loving God, risking your life for some good might require even more courage than if you were confident you will be in a divine paradise after death.

There are classical Christian instructions on the nature of the dark night of the soul (most famously from St. John of the Cross), on how periods of feeling

God's absence can be vital moments of purification, the shedding of self-preoccupation, and a time for courageous, mature growth. The dark night of the soul can be a phase of enormous anguish in which the soul may feel close to oblivion, only to be relieved (at some point) by a profoundly deeper sense of God's presence. Reflections on the fluctuation of sensing God's presence and absence is pervasive in Christian tradition, with biblical roots (see especially theological interpretations of the Song of Songs as an allegory of the soul's relationship with God).

The interior divine presence: We have seen a version of God's omnipresence throughout our cosmos in terms of God's power, knowledge, and goodness, but how might we picture or think about God's interior presence in which God is closer to ourselves than we are? At first glance, this may seem an absurd claim. With physical objects – the table in front of you, for example – it surely makes no sense to think that something can be closer to the table than the table. Why should matters differ when it comes to you and me?

Christian philosophy might make some inroads into this project by highlighting the ways in which persons (unlike tables and rocks) may be remote from themselves. I can be remote or distant from who I am when I have an utterly distorted self-image or self-understanding. Imagine I think of myself as kind and generous, whereas I am actually cruel and miserly, utterly indifferent to the needs of others whom I could assist. There are parts of each of us that we can't help finding elusive: our unconscious, all the truths about our past, the facts about our material well-being (I may think I am healthy but have a weak heart), our communities (you may think you are surrounded by hostile scoundrels when you are actually surrounded by kindhearted friends).

If the God of Christianity exists, God has a closer proximity to ourselves on these fronts than we do. God knows who you think you are – physically and mentally – but God also knows the truth of such matters, as well as your past, your unconscious beliefs and desires, the truths about your community, and more. So far, this is a matter of cognition, but we can also be close to or distant from ourselves affectively. Even if I have an accurate self-understanding, I might be utterly burned out and find myself and others boring, treating life as an ironic game, or, perhaps even worse, I am filled with self-hatred due to ethnic and gender bullying or stereotyping.

We are capable of not just self-deception but also of self-fragmentation when we (wrongly or unjustly) are subject to condemning ourselves or parts of ourselves. In such matters, if the God of Christianity exists, God loves and cares for each of us and seeks to deliver us from evil, both the evil imposed on us from external factors and the evil we ourselves ferment. Perhaps, then, God's interior presence may be understood as God's knowing and willing (desiring) our affective integration, the integration of our actual lives and the lives we might live if unfettered by vice (our own or the vices of others) in a state of flourishing.

Christian philosophy has work to do in order to fill out this portrait. Here are three matters that impact further understanding of God's personal nearness. First, if we adopt the model of God being timelessly eternal, God's proximity to each person encompasses God's knowledge and love of not just what is (for us) past and present but future. Alternatively, in open theism, our future is not yet real and thus not subject to absolutely certain knowledge (divine or human). These two models may lead to different views of prayer and providence.

Second, most Christian philosophy recognizes that God has given free agency (and thus limited autonomy) to created persons and so there is at least one sense in which God is essentially remote from us – God does not make free decisions or choices for us because they would not be free if God controlled them. Perhaps God's nearness to persons might still be real in terms of religious and moral experience (e.g., a wrongdoer might be made aware of the vileness of their act and their obligation to do good), but the whole point of believing in free will is believing that persons can and do freely choose evil, vicious acts. In such acts, we might truly sense God's absence insofar as wrongdoers deviate from God's will.

A third area worth pursuing is to make some sense of persons having a true self or being able to act as we are truly versus relying on deviant, inauthentic desires. Many of us are aware of times when it might be said that we do not seem like ourselves – perhaps when we lose self-control in a crisis or we are drugged or intoxicated. Under such circumstances, God might be experienced as calling us back to our true selves. In this sense, God may be more present to the persons we truly are on occasions when we may be living as distorted versions of who we truly are. These are only sketches of what may be promising future work in Christian philosophy.

3 Is There a Problem with a God's-Eye Point of View?

Sometimes a person will make a moral claim and a critic will object that the person is playing God. Obviously, this is a figure of speech. For a person to try to play God literally – in addition to playing backgammon or tennis – would be quite bizarre, or at least comic; imagine criticizing your discussion partner for trying to create and sustain a cosmos or becoming incarnate in the first century! Presumably, accusing someone of playing God is a colorful way of charging that the person is arrogant or wrongly assuming some titanic, inappropriate authority.

But what about the very idea of a God's-eye point of view? Whether or not there actually is a God, is there something wrong with striving to see moral matters from a divine perspective? And, going further, what if we take seriously the idea that there actually is a God and this God is not morally indifferent and aloof? The God portrayed in Christian tradition is not the God of Aristotle. Unlike Aristotle, Christians attribute love, justice, mercy, providence to God. Does this create problems in Christian philosophy?

One problem facing Christian philosophy involves the relationship of Christian ethics and secular ethics. Arguably, Christian ethicists and secular ethicists (at least in democratic republics) share many values: human persons deserve respect, justice and compassion are good, it is wrong to exploit and manipulate others, self-determination and freedom are good, lying and homicide are wrong (though possibly permitted in special circumstances, as in a just war). But signs of accord have dramatic exceptions.

Here is a partial list of areas where many Christians disagree with each other but also with secular ethicists: racial equality, reparations for past harms, gender equality, marriage, the standing of nonheterosexuality, abortion, euthanasia including physician-assisted suicide, organ transplants, universal healthcare, the distribution of scarce medical resources, famine relief, climate change, socialism versus a free market economy (and variations), the moral standing of nonhuman animals, generational ethics (what does the present generation owe past and future generations?), and more. Sometimes the disputes concern theoretical frameworks. There are Christian and non-Christian utilitarians (consequentialists), Kantians, virtue theorists, advocates of natural law, particularists (those who eschew theory and focus on specific moral judgments), intuitionists, relativists, and contextualists. You would expect that only Christians or theists would accept a divine command theory of ethics (X is good if God approves of it; Y is bad if God disapproves of it), but some atheists are willing to adopt a version of it (X is good if there is a God and God approves of it; Y is bad if there is a God and God disapproves of it).

It would be great if this Element offered solutions to all the problems cited. Or would it? Because such a task would probably be read as my trying to play God, I propose a slightly less daunting endeavor. Let's consider a series of objections to appealing to a God's-eye point of view and then see what might be salvageable or promising about it. But first I offer a brief preface.

Let's use a *God's-eye point of view* to refer to the perspective of a being who has three properties: omniscience of all the facts on the basis of which moral judgments are formed, impartiality (being free of bias or prejudice), and being affectively aware of the points of view of all involved subjects (sometimes called omnipercipience). On the first property, moral judgments are often based on what are believed to be facts. For example, some people judge that carbon emissions should be cut on the basis of what they believe is a fact: current carbon emissions are contributing to climate change, which in turn contributes to ecological disasters, the loss of land and people, droughts, dangerous storms, and so on.

On the second property, impartiality is widely recognized as an essential component in sound moral judgments – being free of bias or prejudice. The third condition reflects an important facet in moral valuations: in forming a moral judgment it is not just a matter of knowing the facts – for example, how many people will die in a drought – it is also a matter of being vividly aware of the suffering involved. For example, someone from a wealthy country who has never experienced famine might be impaired in evaluating the ethics of famine relief because they are ignorant of the effects of famine. Arguably, many disputations in ethics reveal the primacy of these three elements: there are arguments about the facts that provide a basis for moral judgment, parties appeal to impartiality or accuse their opponents of bias, and efforts are made to bring to light the affective dimensions of disputes (e.g., one might well accuse an opponent of being callous emotionally or being clueless about what it feels like to endure racial hatred). A study of these disputations suggests that an ideal moral point of view would involve knowing all the relevant facts, impartiality, and comprehensive affective awareness.

Arguably, the God of Christianity has those three properties: omniscience, impartiality, and omnipresence. Impartiality may seem questionable (doesn't this God have a chosen people?), but apparent partiality has been theologically understood as in service of the greater good, and there are abundant biblical attestations of divine impartiality ("There is no partiality with God" [Romans 2:11]; see also Deuteronomy 10:7, 2 Chronicles 19:7, Psalm 25:8, and Acts 10:31). While the God of Christianity has other properties, those three stand out as explaining why some describe an ideal moral vantage point as a God's-eye point of view. I use the expression "God's-eye point of view" because it is common in the literature, but it is not intended to privilege vision as a cognitive faculty. (Some avoid this worry by referring to ideal observation or to an ideal observer.)

3.1 The Perils of a God's-Eye Point of View

Because the objections considered here run together, I will not enumerate them separately. What follows are problems with appealing to what is believed to be God's revealed will as well as objections to a divine or ideal perspective.

A general, widespread objection to linking morality and theism needs to be registered and then set aside. Some secular critics stress that many nontheists today and historically seem to successfully identify right and wrong, justice and injustice, without any reference to God. It is also claimed that there is no compelling evidence that theists or Christians are more moral than atheists or non-Christians. I note these points, but will set them to one side as many (but not all) Christian philosophers positively affirm that non-Christians are (or can be) aware of moral truths. This affirmation seems supported in the New Testament (Romans 2:15). And few argue that there is compelling evidence that self-identified Christians are more ethical than non-Christians. There are arguments that Christian theism is better able to account for objective moral truths than naturalism (these are often referred to as theistic moral arguments), but these arguments do not rest on either the thesis that only Christians know objective moral truths or the thesis that self-identified Christians are more moral than non-Christians.

A more telling problem concerns caprice and injustice. What should be the response to biblical edicts on dietary laws and rules that seem capricious or cruel (capital punishment for adultery or homosexuality)? And then there is the case of when it appears that God commands the sacrifice of an innocent child; Abraham is commanded to sacrifice his son Isaac in Genesis 22). Such cases seem to undermine reliance on biblical revelation as a guide to ethics.

While impartiality is often considered an ideal judicially (Lady Justice is often depicted with a blindfold, suggesting that justice should be administered without prejudice), it has recently come under fire. Aren't there times when impartiality is not desirable? Think of different stages in the feminist movement or the more recent Black Lives Matter movement. Some complain: don't all lives matter? In response it is held that while it is true that all lives matter, there are times when it is appropriate to focus on specific groups, women and Blacks, especially unarmed Black males who have been victimized by police. Some critics of a God's-eye point of view charge that it encourages detachment. Shouldn't our focus be on oppressed and underrepresented groups rather than striving to be disinterested or not partisan? A great deal of recent Christian ethics appears to agree as Christians today seek to renounce the complicity of self-identified Christians sanctioning slavery and dispossessing indigenous people.

Related to this objection, Pamela Anderson has claimed that the very notion of a God's-eye point of view is gendered. The viewpoint is essentially male, more specifically white, male, and heterosexual. A more mature ethic would be partisan on behalf of those who have suffered oppression, non-white LGBTQ persons especially.

Also under suspicion is the desirability of the affective awareness of all subjects. Is it either necessary or ethically proper to strive to understand the affective lives of rapists, murderers, tyrants? Imagine saying to a child-molesting kidnapper: "I really understand you and your action"? Isn't that tantamount to expressing sympathy (possibly even empathy) with a victimizer?

Finally, the God's-eye point of view ethic has been criticized as providing no motive or grounds for why any person should care what God or an ideal observer thinks. Especially if we bracket the idea that God will judge and punish wrongdoers, why should anyone care what God thinks or values?

3.2 The Promise of a God's-Eye Point of View

On caprice and divine commands that violate our contemporary standards of justice, Christian philosophy has taken different positions. If you adopt the view that the Bible is inerrant, you need to explain why the divinely revealed precepts are justified, at least at the time. Perhaps they are part of God's accommodating the limited, imperfect conditions of the ancient world. Just as it would be odd, and perhaps unintelligible, to convey to ancient people what we know of cosmology and physics, it might be odd to communicate contemporary ethics to people thousands of years ago. Alternatively, some Christian philosophers (especially those who do not embrace biblical inerrancy) propose that what appear to be unjust commands are not God's actual decrees but a people's interpretation of what they thought was just. One principle of interpretation by such Christians is that the Bible as a whole should be interpreted on the basis that God is loving and just. Homosexual Christians point out that the handful of condemnations of homosexuality in the Bible may be due to a condemnation of temple prostitution or rites associated with idolatry. Jesus himself is not recorded as making any negative judgments on single-gendered relations.

Notice that debate over whether homosexual sex can be as healthy as hetero-sexual sex is likely to appeal to the three components of a God's-eye point of view: an appeal to the facts (some have claimed that homosexuality is wrong because it is due to an arrested narcissistic stage of development, it is nonrepro-ductive, and it is almost always the outcome of childhood abuse; each of these reasons has been countered, viz. homosexuality can be the opposite of narcissism, some healthy heterosexual relationships are nonreproductive, and the thesis about child molestation is demonstrably false), impartiality (parties to the debate appeal to reaching a judgment not biased by stereotyping and ingrained prejudice), and affective awareness (try to affectively appreciate what it is like to have this or that sexual orientation). Those who reject biblical prohibitions of homosexuality as authoritative may be understood as arguing that homosexuality can be natural and healthy from a God's-eye point of view (or, putting the matter in reference to theism, an all-good God would not have condemned homosexuality and so the biblical injunctions are not divine decrees, but a matter of human prejudice).

On the story of Abraham and Isaac, some have interpreted Genesis 22 as demonstrating that religious duties can supersede or transcend moral duties, but other readings should be considered. One is that the whole point of the story is that *one ought not to engage in child sacrifice* (after all, God commands that Abraham should not sacrifice Isaac). One might also note that ethics for God can differ from our ethics due to God's power. Being omnipotent, God can raise the dead while we cannot. If Abraham had sacrificed Isaac, God could have instantly restored him to life. A parallel case may be instructive on the different status of God, humans, and property. It would be wrong for me to steal your computer because it belongs to you, not me. But if traditional Christianity (or Judaism or Islam) is true, you, your computer, and the whole creation belongs to God. From that perspective, God cannot steal your computer. More on God and ethics in the next section.

On impartiality, those defending partiality often presuppose that *partiality is proper from an impartial point of view.* Those defending partiality may be understood as arguing that if one is truly impartial, one should see that occasions arise when the primary focus should be on persons who have suffered or been victimized. Being impartial is not the same as being indifferent. Arguably, an impartial observer of unjust police brutality against Blacks would be passionately committed to rectification, punishment of the guilty, taking radical steps to prevent future acts of injustice.

On gender, there is nothing explicitly built into any version of the God's-eye point of view, historically or today, about gender. The God's-eye point of view seems especially well suited to expose cases of the improper introduction of gender bias.

On affective awareness, countless cases may arise when individuals should not seek to affectively grasp the motives of their oppressors. Even so, an expanded affective awareness may be crucial in identifying and preventing future wrongdoing as well as in designing punishment and/or rehabilitation of the guilty. In English, it may be that saying to a kidnapper "I understand why you acted the way you did" is a sign of some sympathy, but there is not an obvious connection between that and condoning the act. Perhaps therapists working with prisoners need to have some sympathy with what drives people to crime in the course of guiding wrongdoers to confession, repentance, moral renewal, seeking forgiveness, and more.

Who cares about a God's-eye point of view? I suggest that anyone who is serious in making a moral claim (e.g., the claim that abortion should be legal in the first trimester of a pregnancy due to rape or incest) is committed to holding that the claim is based on an accurate grasp of the facts, it is made impartially, and it is supported by an awareness of the affective dimension of all involved subjects. It seems incoherent, or at least odd, for someone to advance such a moral claim while also maintaining that the claim would be undermined in light of knowing more facts (e.g., it is actually a fact that such an abortion would involve killing a person), being more impartial (e.g., treating the "fetal person" on the same level as the one who is pregnant), and greater affective awareness (e.g., taking seriously the affective life of the prospective child). In other words, I suggest that when we make moral claims, we are (as it were) wagering that our claims would be supported by a God's-eye point of view, whether or not we believe there is a God or even care whether or not God exists.

If secular and Christian philosophers accept the conditions of the God's-eye point of view, then they can have a shared framework to debate their differences in moral theories and in applied ethics. So debate about moral theory (e.g., utilitarianism) will involve an appeal to the knowledge of facts (the measurement of utility), impartiality (most versions of utilitarianism are averse to privileging self-interest), and affective awareness (does utilitarianism do justice to the affective dimension of the experience of all involved?). Applied ethics will likewise involve the same framework.

3.3 Hazardous Perspectives

The invocation of a God's-eye point of view may shed some light on the problem of evil: if there is an omnipotent, omniscient, all-good God, why is there so much evil? Sometimes the problem of evil is advanced in a way that equates God's ethics with our own. Arguably, if you can prevent a murder, you should do so. If God exists, shouldn't God prevent all murders? Such a question makes sense, but what may be overlooked is that God is not a human bystander, but the creator and sustainer of all of the cosmos. I suggest that the problem of evil needs to be formulated as a question about whether the evils of the cosmos are compatible with the creator and sustainer of the cosmos being the all good God of Christianity. I have characterized a Christian claim about God and evil involving some elements we will cover in the next section (the Trinity, the Incarnation, the afterlife, miracles). Consider the following claim.

It is compatible with the omnipotent, omniscient, supremely good triune God (the apex of the Good, the True, and the Beautiful) to create and sustain a contingent cosmos in which there are stable laws of nature in which there are more than 200 billion galaxies and (virtually) countless stars and planets, at least one of which has produced biota and abiota of plants and animals, some of which are sentient and have powers of thought, memory, reason, emotion, and agency, including moral agency. Living agents engage in good, healthy relations as well as horrific, unhealthy relations.

There are the goods of biological flourishing (respiration, reproduction, and so on), freedom, family, community, and friendship, and grave harms such as murder, rape, oppression, slavery, and tyranny. Murder, rape, oppression, slavery, and tyranny (and more) are contrary to the will and nature of the God who calls all persons to justice, mutual loving compassion, our duty to relieve famines, and so on. God's being is not obvious to creatures, but there are widespread ostensible experiences of God – the appearance of prophets and sages (culminating in the ethical monotheism of the later Hebrew prophets); the incarnation of this God as Jesus of Nazareth who taught nonviolence and the coming of God's Kingdom ultimately through the birth, teaching, suffering, death, and resurrection of Jesus; life after death in which there may be the redemption of wrongdoers who might find fulfillment in union with the triune God of love. God miraculously acts to bring about some goods and prevent some evils (sometimes through human agents; sometimes God acts to relieve famine, sometimes not) in this world, but this is far from obvious and universal. The divine seeking of redemption and justice includes life beyond this life.

This portrait may be filled out on many fronts: some (but not all) Christians are universalists; they believe that all persons will ultimately be saved and brought into harmony with God. While the traditional (and current mainstream) stance is that hell exists as a state of everlasting alienation from God, Christians going back to Origen and Gregory of Nyssa have drawn on such texts as John 12:32, Romans 5:12–21 and 11:32, 1 Timothy 2:4, and others to argue for universalism. Some (but by no means all) Christians believe that some nonhuman animals are ensouled and will survive physical death. However the details are filled out, assessing the problem of evil involves assessing good and evil on a cosmic scale.

Christians may entertain more than one approach to this cosmic picture of God and evil. One may claim to know that God and evil are compatible. As what we call knowledge may suggest a very high degree of certainty, a Christian may, instead of claiming knowledge, claim to have good reason to believe in the compatibility of God and evil. More modestly still, one may claim to have (a reasonable) faith or hope in such compatibility. There is yet another position worthy of note called *skeptical theism*. On this view, it is held that while it is reasonable to believe in the Christian God, we should be skeptics (or agnostics) as to why God does not prevent (more) evil. On the other side, denying that the cosmos is compatible with the existence of a good creator may border on a dark claim to the effect that it would be better if our cosmos did not exist or, even more grim, it might be good if our cosmos perished. Fortunately, there are more moderate positions – it is good that the cosmos exists, but it would be better if there were no horrendous evils. (A minor note on terminology: the term *theodicy* is used for accounts as to why there is evil, while a *defense* refers to making a case that the evils of the cosmos do not logically entail [or make evident] the nonexistence of God.)

Without in any way trying to solve the problem of evil, I suggest that debate about the problem of evil often involves an appeal to a God's-eye point of view. A philosophical atheist who argues that our cosmos is unworthy of being the creation of an all-good God may be likened to someone arguing that such a creation would not occur from the standpoint of omniscience, impartiality, and omnipercipience.

4 Is the God of Christian Philosophy Too Exclusive?

This Element began by noting that "Christian philosophy" is not an everyday term, nor is it included in all current philosophical dictionaries and encyclopedias. Be that as it may, the term is increasingly in use in academic circles. In fact, rather than professional philosophers being baffled by what is Christian philosophy, some claim that there is too much Christian philosophy.

Some contemporary philosophers complain that the majority of issues addressed in philosophy of religion today stem from Christianity. Textbooks, conferences, and multiple journals feature lengthy treatments of the coherence of theism, Christian approaches to epistemology and metaphysics, debate over divine attributes, theistic religious experience, theistic arguments (both historical and novel), atheistic arguments from evil or divine hiddenness, Christian approaches to justice, forgiveness, punishment, mercy, revelation, redemption, miracles, prayer, life after death, race and ethnicity, gender equality, holiness and worship, church and liturgy, and specific Christian doctrinal positions on the Trinity and Incarnation.

Christian applied ethics is also in evidence, especially in medical and environmental ethics. Christian histories of philosophy by Frederick Copleston and C. Stephen Evans, among others, have challenged the near monopoly of histories by Bertrand Russell and William Durant. The standard, canonical 1967 Macmillan *Encyclopedia of Philosophy* edited by Paul Edwards, a polemical atheist, has been superseded by a second edition much more sympathetic to Christian philosophy (the philosophy of religion editors were members of the SCP). The reasons for the apparent domination of Christian philosophy have been debated. Of all the world religions, Christianity is the largest in terms of numbers of adherents. Is it therefore to be expected that greater attention should be directed to the religion with the greatest following on the planet? Have more practicing Christians been attracted to the professional life of philosophy? Whatever the reason, let us first consider the charge that this large-scale attention to Christian philosophy and the God of Christianity is unfortunate. So, is the God of Christian philosophy too exclusive?

4.1 Yes

Pew Research Center estimates that 32 percent of the world's population is Christian (2.2 billion, or roughly three out of ten people are Christian), 23 percent is Muslim, 15 percent is Hindu, and 7 percent is Buddhist. There are also significant numbers of observant Jews along with traditional African religions, Chinese folk religions, Native American religions, and Australian aboriginal religions. There are members of the Baha'i faith, Jainism, Sikhism, Shintoism, Taoism, Tenrikyo, Wicca, and Zoroastrianism, and a growing number of secular, not religiously identified persons. Amid all this religious diversity, shouldn't more philosophical attention spread out to this rich array of traditions? Moreover, some philosophers argue that we should spend more time and energy exploring alternative conceptions of ultimate reality that are not (yet) featured in any extant religions.

On the general topic of exclusivity, the God of Christianity has been historically represented as exclusive in terms of worship and salvation. You should not worship other gods. Faith in Jesus Christ as revealed in the Bible is the only path to salvation. Claims of incarnations, miracles, experiences of the divine, or mystical illumination in other faith traditions are either suspect or ruled out as spurious. As I believe that the objection of exclusivity is both familiar and already summarized in this Element, I concentrate more on how this problem might be addressed in Christian philosophy.

4.2 Not Necessarily

I think there has been a regrettable philosophical neglect of non-Christian religions in the field of philosophy of religion, but one needs to appreciate this in historical context and realize that the intellectual (and academic) climate is changing. Keep in mind that Christianity did not enter the history of philosophy in the West until late antiquity, albeit there was some significant Christian philosophy earlier (there is even a philosophical exchange in Acts 17, cited earlier). In the history of philosophy in the East, Christianity was not a topic until European missionaries introduced Christianity to India, China, and Japan in the Common Era.

Christianity was an important resource for philosophy during the European Enlightenment, not always for advocacy but for a critique that continued into the twentieth century, culminating with post–World War II scientifically oriented philosophy such as logical positivism. With the recession of logical positivism, Christian philosophy underwent a renaissance. At first, this took the form of responding to past critics (Hume, Kant, Feuerbach, Nietzsche, Freud, etc.) and contemporary critics (logical positivists), but by the early 1980s, an astounding outpouring of Christian philosophy was occurring along with a huge wave of interest in non-Christian religions and the topic of religious diversity.

Many Christian philosophers dedicated their professional and personal lives to the exploration and appreciation of non-Christian religious traditions (Ninian Smart, William Wainwright, Chad Meister, to name just a few). One of the barriers to a more global philosophy of religion was surmounted by the greater availability of translations of non-Christian sacred texts and religious philosophy. A major force behind the intense, expanded interest in non-Christian religions was the movement of religious pluralism, spearheaded by British philosopher John Hick, who argued that all world religions are different, equally valid paths to an ultimate divine reality he referred to as the Real. Many of the most recent research tools, such as the magisterial four-volume *Encyclopedia of Philosophy of Religion*, published by Wiley Blackwell in 2021 with more than 450 entries, covers all world religions with many expert scholars who are non-Christian.

While some philosophers lament the centrality of theism in the field of philosophy of religion, it should be appreciated that theism is not exclusive to Christianity. The second largest (and growing dramatically) world religion is theistic: Islam. Judaism has many strands, but it is indisputably a primary historical source for monotheism. There are theistic Hindus, and the Baha'i faith and Sikhism are theistic, as are some traditional African religions. So almost seven out of ten people on the planet have some alignment with theism or been influenced by theistic religion. Moreover, while Confucianism and Taoism are not considered theistic, some scholars see them as compatible with theism. Theism is relevant to Buddhism and Jainism as both religious traditions are anti-theistic (or at least nontheistic). And some forms of Buddhism attribute to the Buddha omniscience (a divine attribute in theistic traditions).

In assessing the standing of Christian philosophy over the past fifty years with multiple new journals, books, societies, centers, and conferences, a principal element is diversity, dispelling the impression that Christian philosophy is homogenous. We have already noted how Christian philosophers have differed on God's relation to time (God being eternal or everlasting – i.e., God is in time but without temporal beginning or end). Now, let us briefly consider accounts of Christianity and science, beliefs about life after death, the Trinity, the Incarnation, salvation and atonement, miracles, and revelation.

What follows is a bare survey to provide evidence of diversity rather than detailed expositions of the alternatives. One takeaway for adult newcomers to Christianity is that if you are curious about Christianity, this is a religion with many nuances to explore. If you are highly critical of Christianity, you may want to question whether you reject only one form of Christianity, and if you already are a Christian with philosophical interests, you have an almost inexhaustible intellectual landscape to investigate.

Christianity and science: While there are still some debates over whether the (presumed truth) of biological evolution is compatible with Christianity, debate has shifted as to whether biological evolution itself calls for a greater philosophical framework to account for stable laws of nature in physics and chemistry; debate over whether secular naturalism can account for the emergence of consciousness, reason, and value; and debate over whether scientific naturalism is self-defeating. Some philosophers maintain that the scientific method can be naturalistic (e.g., not invoking theism) without being committed to the falsity of theism. A better term for the scientific method might be *scientific agnosticism* rather than *scientific atheism*. In Christian philosophy, there are diverse views in philosophy of mind (for humans and nonhuman animals).

Beliefs about life after death: From Christianity's beginning, some Christian philosophers have seen human beings as material creatures. This is often linked with earlier Jewish anthropology in which the life of persons is linked with the breath. But the majority of Christian tradition historically has seen human persons as embodied souls. This is often called *dualism* (a term that meets with great hostility in contemporary accounts of human nature) – the view that while in this life we function as a soul-and-body unity, upon the death of the body, the soul survives, perhaps disembodied or awaiting the resurrection of the body. Today, dualist Christians are rivaled by Christian materialists, who claim their position is more in accord with both the Bible and contemporary science. There are still other accounts, including Christian pan-psychism, according to which all the fundamental components of the physical world have some psychic life.

The Trinity: Historically, Christianity upholds monotheism (there is one God), while also holding that the Godhead is itself not homogenous but consists of three persons – Father, Son, and Holy Spirit. There is a complex biblical and doctrinal story behind the multiple philosophical models of the Trinity, but for reasons of space and simplicity I highlight just two. The so-called Latin model stresses the unity of the divine persons. A strongly unified stance here treats the three divine persons as three modes of God; God is revealed as Father, as Son, and as Holy Spirit. In what is often called *social trinitarianism*, the three persons are three distinct centers of consciousness in co-inherent, perfect union, acting as one in nature. Their co-inherent, loving indwelling is sometimes referred to as *perichoresis* (from the Greek *peri* for "around" and *chorein* for "to give way" or "to make room"). Almost all parties in the current debate wish to avoid tritheism (there are three gods) while respecting the New Testament differentiation of when Jesus prays to the Father (and on the cross suffers a kind of separation from the Father) or when the Holy Spirit is sent to followers of Jesus to dwell within them.

Incarnation: the traditional teaching is that Jesus Christ is wholly human and wholly God. In keeping with different models of the trinity, this involves asserting that while Jesus is *totus Deus* (wholly God), Jesus is not *totum Dei* (the whole of God). This allows for multiple incarnations in other galaxies and times. There are multiple philosophical accounts of the Incarnation. Some involve the second person of the Trinity shedding the divine attributes of omnipotence and omniscience, while others do not. One that does not is sometimes called the *two-minds model*. On this account, the greater mind of the second person of the Trinity retains all divine attributes but creates a finite mind within the greater mind that is born, lives, teaches, suffers, dies, and is resurrected as Jesus of Nazareth.

Salvation and atonement: I observed earlier that some Christians hold that salvation and atonement (at-one-ment with God) can be obtained only through explicit faith in Jesus Christ in this life. Other Christians believe in the Incarnation and work of Jesus as the only means of salvation, but hold that this saving work can be operative either in this life or in life after death. While the New Testament and much of Christian tradition recognizes the reality of hell, some have claimed that the love of God will never abandon created persons to everlasting punishment or separation from God. As one twentieth-century Christian theologian put it, hell may exist, but we must pray that one day it will be empty.

Miracles and revelation: Some Christians hold that miracles and divine revelation are exclusive to the Bible, while other Christian philosophers recognize miracles and revelation in other traditions. Sacred scriptures in non-Christian traditions appear to testify that there is a powerful, loving personal divine reality. Compare, for example, the Gospel of John in the New Testament with the Bhagavad Gita in Hinduism.

While I am painfully aware that this passage may read like a sparse menu due to its compressed brevity, I hope instead that it may be serve as an appetizer prompting you to explore the rich, diverse courses in Christian philosophy that are readily available.

To summarize this section: the purview of philosophy of religion has expanded (and is expanding) to include non-Christian religions. We have seen that other world religions are theistic (e.g., Islam) or have a bearing on theism (Buddhism and Jainism have produced atheistic arguments), and that Christian philosophy is itself not monolithic philosophy but has bolstered significant philosophical diversity.

4.3 Precarious Boundaries

The boundaries between religions can be precarious. Tragically, Christian tradition has included a poisonous anti-Semitism, notwithstanding Jesus and the early disciples being Jews and Christianity's profound Jewish roots. Since the rise of Donald Trump in the United States, there is now a greater realization of how vociferous self-identified Christians foment white supremacy with hateful views of Muslims and non-white peoples (whether those people claim to also be Christian or not). In some Islamic countries, it is impermissible for a Muslim to convert to another religion. Sharia allows non-Muslims to convert to Islam but conversion to Christianity has been viewed as a form of apostasy.

Rather than use this section to chronicle the ills and benefits (the bad and good problems) within or between Christianity and other religions, I offer seven guidelines for debate and criticism that are inspired by Christian teachings. The final part of this section is thus intended to provide steps for reducing bad problems in Christian philosophy.

In what follows, I advance six steps: I suggest that those who practice Christian philosophy give primacy to loving the good rather than loathing the evil in their own and other religious communities; that self-criticism should have priority over any criticism of other persons or traditions; a philosophical golden rule should be observed; schism and persecution should be avoided; Christians need to be open to criticism from non-Christian sources; and there are reasons to practice being philosophical Good Samaritans.

I. The primacy of loving the good. Sadly, the criticism of some Christians of non-Christian religions focuses on dubious, not central cases, as when an objection to Islam takes aim at Wahhabism (founded in the eighteenth century by Muhammad ibn Abd al-Wahhab), an extremist group that promotes terrorism, forgetting the massive commitment to justice in the Quran and Islamic tradition. On the other hand, some critiques of Christianity focus on the Crusades, the witch craze in Europe, or the trial of Galileo, forgetting that the Crusades were highly complex (some of it was a defensive response to Ottoman aggression); there were Christians at the time who advocated good magic (the Florentine Academy under Ficino) and Christians who accepted heliocentricity and embraced modern science. Such a focusing first and foremost on what is believed to be wrong about one's interlocuter can be dangerous and distorting.

In *The Genealogy of Morality*, Friedrich Nietzsche (1994) contends that sometimes a religious or moral stance can appear to be based on positive values when, in reality, the stance is based on envy and resentment. In my view, while in the book *Ressentiment* Max Scheler (1994) has shown that at least some Christian values are thoroughly positive, Nietzsche's analysis should prompt

Christians to ensure that their use of criticism (of fellow Christians or non-Christians) should be primarily motivated by a love and the good. There are abundant biblical precepts to the effect that evil is to be overcome not with evil, but with goodness (Romans 12:21, 1 Thessalonians 5:15, Galations 5:22). We are told to love enemies (Matthew 5:4) and that hating others puts us at enmity with God (1 John 3:15).

By stressing the primacy of love, the good one will naturally be led positively to purify the motives behind the criticism. This would involve the renunciation of vices such as vanity (the inordinate desire for preeminence), malice, jealousy, envy, resentment, (inappropriate) anger, or rage. Scheler appropriately points out one of the dangers of motives for morality that privilege hate more than love. Consider a police officer who is principally motivated by her hatred of injustice or a doctor who hates disease. Scheler proposes that in both cases, the agents' lives are defined by what they oppose, so much so that if there were no injustice or illness, their lives would lack meaning. Their lives are, in a sense, parasitic on that which they despise. Far better, according to Scheler, for the officer to love justice and the doctor to love health. The officer and doctor may still hate injustice and illness, but this is best rooted in a deeper love for justice and health.

Perhaps an example closer to home for some readers would be to compare a teacher who loves wisdom and knowledge with a teacher who principally hates foolishness and ignorance. I would prefer the first as I imagine the teacher who loves wisdom and knowledge taking pleasure in the growth of her students, while the other teacher becomes less loathing as his students become less foolish and ignorant. In religious dialogue and debates with secular philosophers, there are reasons from within Christian tradition to first highlight what is good in the interlocutor's worldview. Christian philosophers may praise secular naturalists for their commitment to science, love of truth, and integrity.

II. The importance of self-criticism prior to the criticism of others. Perhaps the clearest New Testament admonition to prioritize self-evaluation is Matthew 7:3–5: "And why do you look at the speck in your brother's eye, but do not notice the log that is in your own eye?" Interestingly, Jesus does not undermine the motive of a brother to assist a brother in correction or healing, but only after the one seeking to aid the other undergoes self-examination and self-purification: "Or how can you say to your brother, 'Let me take the speck out of your eye,' and behold the log is in your eye? You hypocrite, first take the log out of your own eye; and then you will see clearly enough to take the speck out of your brother's eye" (Matthew 7:3).

Confessing one's sins, in both the Old Testament and the New, is a colossal element in a redeemed, reconciliatory relationship with creatures and Creator.

Some of the cases of sinners calling on Christ for mercy are likely the foundation for the Jesus Prayer in wide use in Eastern Orthodox churches: "Lord Jesus Christ, Son of God, have mercy on me, a sinner." The Lord's Prayer (Matthew 6:9–13; Luke 11:2–4) enjoins practitioners first to acknowledge their own sins (trespasses, faults) and then to observe or reflect on the extent to which they have forgiven those who have sinned against them. In fact, the prayer gauges the supplication for forgiveness to the extent that the supplicant practices forgiveness. These practices are evidence of the priority of individual self-scrutiny and of admitting one's own sin.

III. The Golden Rule. I suggest that a third principle guiding criticism from a Christian point of view should involve the Golden Rule – doing to others what you would have them do to you (Matthew 7:12). If you do not want your own religion treated with hostility and derision, don't treat the religions of others with contempt.

In *The City of God*, Augustine records a fellowship he had with his friends in which disagreements were treated with the greatest care for everyone's mutual benefit. The following, from Augustine's *Confessions*, may serve as an ideal case of treating others with mutual care:

> There were joys to be found in their company which still more captivated my mind – the charms of talking and laughing together and kindly giving way to each other's wishes, reading elegantly written books together, sharing jokes and delighting to honour one another, disagreeing occasionally but without rancour, as a person might disagree with themselves, and lending piquancy by that rare disagreement to our much more frequent accord. We would teach and learn from each other, sadly missing any who were absent and blithely welcoming them when they returned. Such signs of friendship sprang from the hearts of friends who loved and knew their love returned, signs to be read in smiles, words, glances and a thousand gracious gestures. So were sparks kindled and our minds were fused inseparably, out of many becoming one. (1961: 79)

(IV) The avoidance of schism and persecution. Obviously, criticism of another person or group sometimes does not remain peaceful; it can be a prelude to divorce, expulsion from a community, the declaration that a former "believer" is now an apostate, condemnation, or violence. Tragically, criticism in the history of Christianity has played such ugly roles. This may seem surprising given the New Testament teaching on peace and peacemaking (e.g., "Blessed are the peacemakers" [Matthew 5:9]), the call for forbearance (Galatians 5:22), the command to forgive others (Matthew 18:21–22), the value of not being divided (Matthew 12:22–28; Mark 3:25), and so on. There have been historically pacifist churches, and, in fact, the early church was ambivalent about whether Christians could serve in the military. Still, Christ cleansed the

temple (Matthew 21:12–17), and one needs to balance a verse like "Put away your sword" (Matthew 26:52) with others ("Think not that I come to send peace on earth. I am not to send peace, but a sword" [Matthew 10:34]). The church was persecuted at its inception (and is still persecuted in places), but Christians and their churches have themselves engaged in persecution and violence. Think of the Inquisition and witch trials, the abundant cases when, historically, so-called Christians killed Christians in the great religious wars of Europe, including the sacking of Constantinople during the Fourth Crusade, and there had been shameful, great violence against Jews by so-called Christians prior to World War II. Think also of the beheading of Thomas More by a Protestant king, as well as of the burning of the Oxford Martyrs by a Roman Catholic monarch, the burning of Bruno, and so on.

Looking over such a tragic history, one needs to appreciate how destructive all such violence in the name of Christianity has been. I suggest the historical legacy of such violence needs to caution the Christian practice of criticism. In the contemporary context, when non-Christian groups have been persecuted, dispossessed, and vulnerable to violence, philosophical and theological criticism of the relevant non-Christian traditions needs either to cease altogether or to be suspended until stable, just conditions are established. When groups are in a crisis, it is time for Christians to show solidarity with the oppressed, regardless of whether or not this involves protecting communities who may be quite hostile to Christianity.

(V) Openness to criticism from non-Christian sources. Earlier, I referred to Nietzsche's *The Genealogy of Morality.* While I believe Scheler successfully rebutted Nietzsche's claim that Christianity is based on negative emotions (such as envy and resentment), I suggest that it is vital for Christians to take seriously such charges, as well as the criticism of Christian beliefs and values from a variety of perspectives (that of Karl Marx, Freud, non-Christian feminists, environmentalists, advocates of race theory, and more). Not all criticism of Christianity is well motivated or fair; some of the critiques by so-called New Atheists seem wide of their mark. However, their work has led many Christian philosophers to publish excellent responses to Richard Dawkins et al.

The most engaging and dramatic moment in terms of the Christian community in the United States responding to external criticism involves the environmental movement, which began in the 1960s and still has momentum today. From the movement's inception, environmentally oriented philosophers and ethicists blamed Christianity for fostering a view of nature in which the natural world was deemed a realm in which humans may dominate without seeing nature (including all nonhuman animals) as valuable for its own sake. The case against Christianity is abundant among philosophical environmentalist (Paul Taylor, J. Baird Collicott, et al.), but nowhere more explicit and articulate than in a famous article, "The Historical Roots of Our Environmental Crisis" by Lynn White in 1967, widely anthologized in environmental ethics textbooks. Regardless of whether White (1907–1987) was himself a Christian, the article encapsulated the judgment of non-Christians who saw Christianity as dangerous and to blame for Western exploitation of the natural world.

White's essay stimulated a massive, creative response from Christian philosophers and theologians who sought to find the resources within Christianity to recognize and treasure the innate goodness of the created world. A kind of green Christian ecological movement and literature came about with contributors including Wendell Berry, Wes Jackson, Robin Attfield, Holmes Rolston III, Andrew Linzey, and many others. Linzey, an Anglican priest, founded a Christian vegetarian movement, as well as the Oxford Centre for Animal Ethics. Linzey and others acknowledged the legitimacy of the critique of how Christian tradition had been used to exploit the natural world, and yet they urged that Christianity had great resources to condemn such exploitation and to provide a theological foundation for environmentalism.

A model of a critical engagement by a major twentieth-century atheist and the Christian community is Albert Camus's presentation in 1948 to a Dominican monastery on what the world expects of Christians. Camus calls on Christians to be in solidarity with all who oppose violence against children and human persons in general. While positive in tone and substance, the talk and subsequently published paper may be read as cajoling Christians who do not recognize or act on their obligation to such solidarity. Here are the opening comments:

> Inasmuch as you have been so kind as to invite a man who does not share your convictions to come and answer the very general question that you are raising in these conversations, before telling you what I think unbelievers expect of Christians, I should like first to acknowledge your intellectual generosity.
>
> I shall strive not to be the person who pretends to believe that Christianity is an easy thing and asks of the Christian, on the basis of an external view of Christianity, more than he asks of himself. I believe indeed that the Christian has many obligations but that it is not up to the man who rejects them himself to recall their existence to anyone who has already accepted them. If there is anyone who can ask anything of the Christian, it is the Christian him/herself . . .
>
> What the world expects of Christians is that Christians should speak out, loud and clear, and that they should voice their condemnation in such a way that never a doubt, never the slightest doubt, could rise in the heart of the simplest man. That they should get away from abstraction and confront the blood-stained face history has taken on today. The grouping we need is a grouping of men/women resolved to speak out clearly and to pay up personally. (Camus, 2010)

This case is profoundly different from the current rhetoric by New Atheists blaming Christians (and other theists) of mindlessly cultivating delusions and so on.

(VI) Good Samaritan virtue. The parable of the Good Samaritan, which appears in Luke 10:25–29, is about a stranger who comes to the aid of a traveler who has been beaten and robbed. The rescuer, a Samaritan, provides direct care and even pays for refuge for the victim to recover. I suggest that there can arise cases when a non-Christian person or community is unfairly and cruelly criticized by others when a Christian can and should intervene. Imagine a Muslim community in a country that is largely non-Muslim is being wrongly criticized for being superstitious and, for whatever reason (a language barrier or culturally embedded Islamophobia), the community lacks the resources to effectively rebut the criticism. If a Christian person or community can effectively protect the Muslim community, I believe it is their Good Samaritan obligation to do so. There may be inappropriate ways to provide aid (e.g., through condescension or patronizing), but it seems to me that such aid might be done without vice and perhaps even involve courage on behalf of the Christian.

My hope is that these guidelines will prove useful in Christian and non-Christian philosophy. Because one of the precepts is to confess one's own shortcomings, I confess that I have come to value these guidelines the hard way, through a humbling (sometimes humiliating) realization of my own shortcomings.

5 God: Good and Bad Problems

At the outset of this Element, I cited Bertrand Russell's claim that philosophy itself emerges when we run into problems about justifying our knowledge of the world. Looking at what may be called a philosophy of problems, the history of philosophy, West and East, may be understood in terms of a series of questions and proposed answers or, rephrasing this slightly, a series of problems and proposed solutions.

Such questions or problems have included ontology (What is there? What is its origin and future? Who and what are we? Is there some kind of divine or sacred reality such as God or gods or Brahman or Tao?), epistemology (What can we know or reasonably believe? What methods of inquiry can lead us to true beliefs?), and values (What is right or wrong? Good or bad? Beautiful or ugly? Sacred or profane?), including matters of governance (How should we live socially? What principles should govern lawmaking?). And there are almost uncountably many questions or potential problems in virtually all the subdisciplines of philosophy: logic and the philosophy of mathematics, philosophy of art, philosophy of history, and, of course, the philosophy of religion.

In this section, I offer a modest guide to good and bad philosophical problems, especially as this bears on Christian philosophy and the problem of God. I then return to the problem of evil and when this problem might be good or bad. I end with reflections on when, if ever, it is philosophically legitimate to appeal to mystery.

5.1 A Modest Guide to Philosophical Problems

Some problems that might have a bearing on Christian philosophy seem to be past, such as finding the physical location of Eden or Noah's ark (perhaps on Mount Ararat?) or dating the creation of the cosmos based on biblical data or predicting the Second Coming (Pope Innocent III thought it would occur in the year 666; Martin Luther thought it would happen before 1600). But all the topics raised so far in this Element (theistic arguments, divine attributes, the problem of evil, religious diversity, and so on) are alive today, receiving significant philosophical attention, whether such attention is enthusiastic or vexatious or somewhere in between.

One approach to philosophical problems that is helpful involves clarifying the background framework and the status of the assumptions that are being employed. Consider an example outside the philosophy of religion. For more than two hundred years, some philosophers have struggled with the problem of a supposed fact–value bifurcation. As it is sometimes put: How can one infer an "ought statement" from an "is statement"? It is one thing to say "Jones killed Smith" and another thing to say "Jones ought not to have killed Smith." In some circles, it is still said that to infer an ought statement from an is statement is to commit the naturalistic fallacy.

But for at least fifty years, this framework and its assumption(s) have been questioned. Is there really a radical difference between facts and values? Arguably, many factual statements are laden with values – for example, Jones is suffering from bone cancer, Smith went blind after being tortured, Williams gave birth to a happy child. A competent user of the English language would not understand these factual observations without realizing that suffering from bone cancer and going blind from torture were bad for Jones and Smith and giving birth to a healthy child was good for Williams and the child.

We can, of course, muddy the waters by imagining various additional facts – for example, maybe Jones got bone cancer from the misfiring of a radiation bomb he constructed to destroy London and the cancer prevented him from making another weapon of mass destruction. But even such an addendum presupposes there is no obvious fact–value bifurcation. A supposed bifurcation seems even more dubious when it is appreciated that the recognition of facts involves the exercise of epistemic values – for example, one ought to believe what is evident.

I suggest that identifying bona fide philosophical problems and their proposed solutions should be guided by what seems evident. One can always dissolve the fact–value bifurcation by claiming that there are no facts. Apart from risking incoherence (viz. it is a fact that there are no facts), the denial that there are facts would be as plausible as denying that persons exist or that there is an external world (versus we are all only dreaming). Being guided by (presumptive) evidence allows us to untangle some knotty problems of the past. For example, consider the charge that it is problematic to believe that persons have free will in light of deterministic science. Belief in free will may still be problematic, but today, it is widely (but not universally) believed that science is not deterministic.

Problems in the philosophy of God are not exactly in the eye of the beholder (so to speak), but they will vary depending upon the framework and assumptions about what is evident. If you are absolutely convinced of the truth of nominalism, you will not think that God's sovereignty is compromised by the existence of necessarily existing, uncreated, Platonic abstract objects. To further chart the difference between good and bad problems, consider again the problem of evil.

5.2 God's Problems and Human Problems

The theistic problem of evil is serious. If God is the all-good, omnipotent, omniscient, loving creator and sustainer of the cosmos, why is there so much evil? Some evils may stem from some goods like the existence of free will in the course of persons being accountable for the well-being of others, or stable laws of nature enabling the emergence of conscious life, and so on. Moreover, I suggested that assessing the problem of evil calls for a God's-eye point of view rather than treating God anthropomorphically as a fellow creature. This greater point of view allows one to take into account Christian beliefs about revelation, the Incarnation, life after death, and more. In this section, I offer three further observations; the first two are ostensibly bad problems.

The problem of evil as a bad human problem. I suggest that a Christian approach to the problem of evil would take a bad turn if it in any way reduced the horror of evil. While the Christian vision of redeeming wrongdoers (either in this life or the next) may be a recognizable good, it should not (in my view) lead us to think that the evils of the cosmos are good or justified. Rather, in God's creation, murder, rape, torture, and so on are profound evils against the nature and will of God. A related, but even worse outcome is if the Christian approach to the problem of evil relaxed or lessened the vital human obligation to prevent evil whenever we can do so (without creating a greater evil).

The problem of evil as a bad divine problem. While some Christian philosophers may disagree, I suggest that it is not desirable to view the God of Christianity as somehow above morality (or as amoral), indifferent to the creation, or to hold that God is a complex mix of good and evil. At least one prominent Christian philosopher argues that morality is a matter of being accountable to a sovereign power with laws, whereas there is no sovereign above God. I submit that this is too wide a divergence from the Bible and Christian tradition that understands God to be just and merciful, a God of love. It is hard to take seriously the biblical and liturgical invocation to delight in and adore the God of love if God is utterly indifferent to the ills of the cosmos.

Assuming the first two problems are avoided, I suggest that there is one desirable problem of evil, namely it is good that evil is a problem (evil should not occur) as opposed to evil being a natural, expected element in the cosmos. Some naturalists propose that while what we categorize as evil are aberrations or abominations from the standpoint of Christian philosophy, they are fully accommodated (not in the sense of welcomed, but in terms of explained) in a cosmos in which there is "blind nature" (to use David Hume's vivid term) as opposed to a God of love. Seeing evil as a problem in a theistic cosmos can strengthen the resolve to fight evil and to give hope that the omnipotent, loving God of the Christian faith will redeem wrongdoers and heal the victims of evil.

Please take note: I am not suggesting that secular naturalists will tend to be less appalled by cosmic evils than Christian philosophers or more ready to accommodate murder and so on. I am, however, proposing that Christian theism sees evil as a profound abuse of the purpose of creation, a truly shocking sin or sacrilege against God, the creator and sustainer of all. Secular naturalism does not, nor does it offer the prospects of a life after our death in which there might be a great redemption of wrongdoers and their victims.

5.3 Mystery: A Modest Guide

Some philosophers have claimed that there is a time to stop practicing philosophy. Perhaps the most famous twentieth-century philosopher to do this was Austria-born Ludwig Wittgenstein, who worked mostly in Britain. He claimed to have solved or, more accurately, dissolved all interesting philosophical problems. Few philosophers today agree that Wittgenstein succeeded. On the contrary, it seems more clear that occasions arise when philosophers stop practicing philosophy too soon. Imagine a behaviorist philosopher who dismisses any recognition that we are conscious, experiencing subjects who can reliably introspect when we are in severe pain. Few of us would be content with the behaviorist telling us that our apparent sense of severe pain is a mystery, an odd illusion we should ignore because it does not fit into a behaviorist account of human nature. But consider a different candidate as a mystery: the God of Christian philosophy.

As I hope is clear, there is a great deal of philosophical work in Christian philosophy, today and for two thousand years, on the divine attributes, the Bible, theistic arguments (although we have not examined specific arguments like the cosmological arguments, we have noted that evidentialism runs throughout Christian philosophy), God's transcendence and omnipresence, the God's-eye point of view, God and ethics, the problem of evil, the diversity of Christian philosophy on the Trinity, the Incarnation, religious diversity, and more.

Still, most philosophies ask us to accept some terms or events as basic and not further explained in other terms and events. For example, Plato and Aristotle ask us to accept the reality of substances or things, like you and me. They claim (with good reason) to distinguish substances from their properties (I had the property of *being a student* and now have the property of *being a philosophy professor*), and a Platonist or Aristotelian can go on to elucidate the differences between a substance and a relation (being a sibling), a process (being cared for by a nurse with a Platonic tattoo), an abstract object (the idea of justice), periods of time (the year 2030), and so on. Even so, the reality of substances like you and me is philosophically foundational. You may choose a different foundation, perhaps subatomic particles, but I wager that in the course of explaining your alternative framework, you will be assuming some kind of basic thing or category, not accounted for by some deeper, further thing or category.

From the standpoint of the perfect being tradition in Christian philosophy, a fundamental feature of God as the maximally (unsurpassably) great reality is God being a causally efficacious, necessarily existing reality. God's necessity is not a complete mystery in terms of being utterly opaque. We may say that a necessarily existing being is noncontingent, a reality that cannot not exist, a being whose nonexistence is impossible. I further suggest that we can give examples of necessarily existing things (the proposition that $1+1=2$) and that (in light of one plausible cosmological argument) our contingent cosmos is not ultimately explainable if there is no causally efficacious necessarily existing being. Still, the reality of God as a necessarily existing reality is not accountable in terms of some supposed deeper reality, like a superior God, or the categories of our minds or a reflection of human language and culture.

Is that (or would that be) a problem? If Christian philosophy does have reason to recognize the reality of a not further explainable divine reality, the language of problems and (possible) solutions seems (to me) inappropriate. French

Christian philosopher Gabriel Marcel distinguished philosophical problems from mystery. There is not the space to critically explain and engage his work here, but I will draw on one of his suggestions:

> A problem is something which I meet, which I find completely before me, but which I can therefore lay siege to and reduce. But a mystery is something in which I am myself involved, and it can therefore only be thought of as a sphere where the distinction between what is in me and what is before me loses its meaning and initial validity. (Marcel 1949, p. 117)

If the reality of the God of Christian philosophy is acknowledged, then what might make recognizing the reality of that God as more of a mystery than a problem is that it invites a personal exploration involving the meaning of one's life. True, that exploration may involve practices that are different from the conventions of mainline secular philosophy. And yet, contra Bertrand Russell and his followers, it need not prevent one from fully participating in the life of philosophy today with its many journals, conventions, societies, and books.

References

Anonymous (2009) *Cloud of Unknowing*. Orleans, MA: Paraclete Press.

Antony, Louise (ed.) (2010) *Philosophers without Gods: Meditations on Atheism and the Secular Life*. Oxford: Oxford University Press.

Augustine, Saint (1961) *Confessions*, translated by R. S. Pine-Coffin. London: Penguin.

   (2004) *The City of God*, Translated by Henry Bettenson. Westminster: Penguin.

Balthasar, Hans U. von (1982) *The Glory of the Lord: A Theological Aesthetics*. San Francisco, CA: San Francisco Press.

Buber, Martin (1970) *I and Thou*, translated by W. Kaufman. New York: Scribner's Sons.

Camus, A. (2010) http://epicblogerin.blogspot.com/2010/05/what-camus-expects-of-christians.html.

Clifford, W. K. (1877 [1999]) "The Ethics of Belief." In *The Ethics of Belief and Other Essays*, edited by T. Madigan. Amherst, MA: Prometheus Press. 70–96.

Creel, Richard E. (1984) "Philosophy's Bowl of Pottage: Reflections on the Value of Faith." *Faith and Philosophy: Journal of the Society of Christian Philosophers* 1:2, Article 8, 230–235.

   (1986) *Divine Impassibility*. Cambridge: Cambridge University Press.

Forrest, B. K., J. D. Chatraw, and A. McGrath (eds.) (2002) *History of Apologetics*. Grand Rapids, MI: Zondervan.

Gilson, Étienne. 1955. *History of Christian Philosophy in the Middle Ages*. Washington, DC: Catholic University of America Press.

Goetz, Stewart, and Charles Taliaferro (2008) *Naturalism*. Grand Rapids, MI: Eerdmans.

Goetz, Stewart, and Charles Taliaferro (eds.) (2021) *Encyclopedia of Philosophy of Religion*. Oxford: Wiley-Blackwell.

Hadot, Pierre (1995) *Philosophy As a Way of Life: Spiritual Exercises from Socrates to Foucault*, translated by M. Chase. Oxford: Blackwell.

Le Poidevin, Robin (2023) *And Was Made Man: Mind, Metaphysics, and Incarnation*. Oxford: Oxford University Press.

Lycan, William (2019) *On Evidence in Philosophy*. Oxford: Oxford University Press.

Marcel, Gabriel (1949) *Being and Having*, translated by Katharine Farrer. Westminster: Dacre Press.

McCabe, Herbert (2002) *God Still Matters*. London: Continuum.

Morris, T. V. (ed.) (1996) *God and the Philosophers*. Oxford: Oxford University Press.

National Academy of Sciences and Institute of Medicine (NASIM) (2008) *Science, Evolution, and Creationism*, third edition. Washington, DC: National Academies Press. https://doi.org/10.17226/11876.

Nietzsche, F. (1994) *On the Genealogy of Morality*. Cambridge: Cambridge University Press.

Phillips, D. Z. (1970) *Faith and Philosophical Enquiry*. London: Routledge.

Plantinga, Alvin (1984) "Advice to Christian Philosophers." *Faith and Philosophy* 1:3, 253–271.

(2015) *Knowledge and Christian Belief*. Grand Rapids, MI: Eerdmans.

Pseudo-Dionysius (1987) *The Complete Works*, translated by C. Luibeid. New York: Paulist Press.

Russell, Bertrand (1912) *The Problems of Philosophy*. www.gutenberg.org/files/5827/5827-h/5827-h.htm.

(2009) *The Basic Writings of Bertrand Russell*, edited by R. E. Enger and L. E. Denonn. London: Routledge.

Schellenberg, J. L. (2019) "Is Plantinga's Style of Christian Philosophy Really Philosophy?" In *Christian Philosophy*, edited by J. A. Simmons. Oxford: Oxford University Press, chapter 13.

Scheler, Max (1994) *Ressentiment*, translated by L. B. Coser. Milwaukee, WI: Marquette University Press.

Searle, John (2007) *Freedom and Neurobiology*. New York: Columbia University Press.

Taliaferro, Charles (1994) *Consciousness and the Mind of God*. Cambridge: Cambridge University Press.

(2005) *Evidence and Faith*. Cambridge: Cambridge University Press.

(2012) *The Golden Cord: A Short Book on the Secular and the Sacred*. Notre Dame, IN: University of Notre Dame Press.

(2019) "Philosophy of Religion." *Stanford Encyclopedia of Philosophy*. https://plato.stanford.edu/entries/philosophy-religion.

(2021) *Religions: A Quick Immersion*. New York: Tibidabo Press.

Taliaferro, C., and Thomas Churchill (2015) "Is Strategic Thinking Desirable in Philosophical Reflection?" *Philosophia Christi* 17:1, 213–221.

Taliaferro, C., and Elizabeth Duel (2011) "Testimony, Evidence and Wisdom in Today's Philosophy of Religion." *Teaching Philosophy* 34:2, 105–118.

Taliaferro, Charles, and Elsa Marty (eds.). (2018) *A Dictionary of Philosophy of Religion*. London: Bloomsbury.

Taliaferro, C., and Mark Odden (2012) "Tattoos and the Tattooing Arts in Perspective." In *Tattoos: Philosophy for Everyone. I Ink, Therefore I am*, edited by Robert Arp. Oxford: Wiley-Blackwell, chapter one.

Van de Weyer, Robert (ed.) (1997) *Harper Collins Book of Prayers*. San Francisco, CA: Harper Collins.

White, Lynn (1967) "The Historical Roots of our Ecological Crisis." *Science* 155, 1203–1207.

Acknowledgments

I am immensely grateful to Michael Peterson for inviting me to contribute to this series, to two anonymous reviewers, and to Felinda Sharmal. Paul Reasoner offered outstanding advice on the project. For reflection on Christian philosophy, I am indebted to many students and professional philosophers, including Marilyn Adams, Lynne Baker, Paul Draper, Stewart Goetz, Douglas Hedley, Jason Marsh, Chad Meister, Phil Quinn, Aaron Simmons, Keith Ward, Mark Wynn, and Linda Zagzebski. I began this book while I was in the process of recovering from a medical crisis; I would not have healed without the loving support of Jil Evans, the love of my life, American painter, coauthor. Thanks also to Brooke White and Julia Fischer for essential physical therapy and much-needed humor.

Cambridge Elements $\equiv$

The Problems of God

Series Editor

Michael L. Peterson
Asbury Theological Seminary

Michael Peterson is Professor of Philosophy at Asbury Theological Seminary.
He is the author of *God and Evil* (Routledge); *Monotheism, Suffering, and Evil*
(Cambridge University Press); *With All Your Mind* (University of Notre Dame Press);
C. S. Lewis and the Christian Worldview (Oxford University Press); *Evil and the Christian God*
(Baker Book House); and *Philosophy of Education: Issues and Options* (Intervarsity Press).
He is co-author of *Reason and Religious Belief* (Oxford University Press); *Science, Evolution,
and Religion: A Debate about Atheism and Theism* (Oxford University Press); and *Biology,
Religion, and Philosophy* (Cambridge University Press). He is editor of *The Problem
of Evil: Selected Readings* (University of Notre Dame Press). He is co-editor of *Philosophy of
Religion: Selected Readings* (Oxford University Press) and *Contemporary Debates in
Philosophy of Religion* (Wiley-Blackwell). He served as General Editor of the Blackwell
monograph series Exploring Philosophy of Religion and is founding Managing
Editor of the journal *Faith and Philosophy.*

About the Series

This series explores problems related to God, such as the human quest for God or
gods, contemplation of God, and critique and rejection of God. Concise, authoritative
volumes in this series will reflect the methods of a variety of disciplines, including
philosophy of religion, theology, religious studies, and sociology.

Cambridge Elements ≡

The Problems of God

Elements in the Series

A full series listing is available at: www.cambridge.org/EPOG

Printed in the United States
by Baker & Taylor Publisher Services